Cattern Cakes
and Lace

D1340732

A CALENDAR OF FEASTS

Cattern Cakes and Lace

JULIA JONES and **BARBARA DEER**

DORLING KINDERSLEY
LONDON

To Matthew, Esther and Katie – with our love

EDITOR Joanna Lorenz
DESIGNED BY Peter Bridgewater Associates
DESIGNERS Peter Bridgewater and Linda Moore
EDITORIAL DIRECTOR Jill Norman
PHOTOGRAPHY Larry Bray
ILLUSTRATED BACKGROUNDS Katy Sleight

First published in Great Britain in 1987 by
DORLING KINDERSLEY LIMITED
9 Henrietta Street
London WC2E 8PS

First paperback edition published in 1991

BRITISH LIBRARY CATALOGUING IN PUBLICATION DATA

Jones, Julia
Cattern cakes and lace: a calendar of traditional festivals
and food.
1. Festivals of Great Britain
I. Title
790.1   GT4843

ISBN 0-86318-252-6

TYPESET BY Central Southern Typesetters, Eastbourne
PRINTED AND BOUND in Spain by Graficromo, S.A., Cordoba

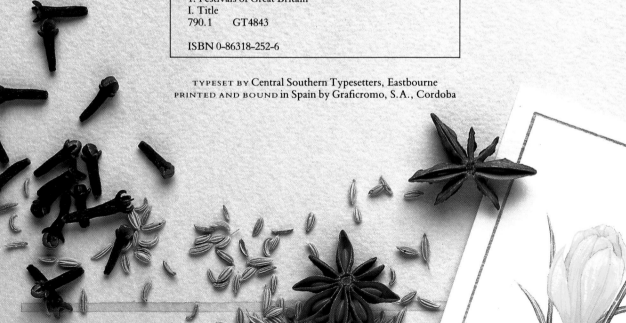

Contents

Preface

This is a cookery book – but not exactly. It is a scrapbook of recipes, folklore and snippets of poetry and handicrafts, much of which has been hammering for some time on my brain, waiting to get out and be acknowledged. The spark came whilst reading a book on lacemaking (a subject on which I wax lyrical), when mention was made of the lacemakers in Tudor times, celebrating the feast of their patron saint, St. Catherine, with Cattern cakes and bohea tea. This information set the seeds in my mind for this book. I am no expert on lacemaking, history or cookery – yet this book contains information on all three. I am more a magpie, collecting gems of knowledge – these I have assembled in a manner pleasing to me and, I hope, to you.

The Cattern cakes of the title I have already explained, and the recipe for these will be found amongst these pages, together with bobbins and samples of lace such as those lacemakers long ago would have fashioned and by which they earned their meagre livings.

In modern towns, the seasons now melt into one another, but I believe that men and women still need to be in touch with the rhythm of life and experience the changes in the cycle of the year. Nothing is more satisfying than following the paths of our forefathers, continuing the traditions handed on to us. I feel great contentment when preparing for my family a dish that my grandmother made for hers, and, I hope, in turn my daughter will make those dishes and tell the same stories for her family.

I start my trip through a British year of cookery and traditional celebrations on November 25th with Cattern cakes on St. Catherine's day, and follow with the run-up to Christmas and the New Year. I hope you will, whatever time you read this book, follow (as I do) the celebrations throughout the year, adding to them your own special touches and enjoying the fruits of each season.

NOVEMBER 25

St. Catherine's Day

CATTERN CAKES (so called after a corruption of the name Catherine) were, as I explained in the preface, the unlikely catalyst that produced this book, bringing together as they do my interest in festivals, food and lacemaking.

St. Catherine of Alexandria, reputedly one of the most intelligent and beautiful women of her day, was martyred in 310 A.D. Her fame reached Europe with the returning Crusaders and the Catherine Wheel firework and Catherine or Rose window were named after her.

St. Catherine was taken up as the protector of young unmarried girls, and it was believed that maidens in need of a husband could crown her statue with a wreath of greenery on this day for their prayers to be answered. The wheel of her death also became the emblem of spinners and lacemakers, for whom St. Catherine became a patron saint. On her day, lacemakers would hold their annual holiday.

St. Catherine's Day was also chosen to honour good Queen Katherine of Aragon, who was patron of local lacemakers during her imprisonment at Ampthill. The story goes that the Queen, after hearing the sad plight of the women of Bedfordshire, ordered all her lace to be burned and commissioned new, in order to give work to the local industry. A certain bobbin lace was named 'Katherine of Aragon's lace' after her, and, thereafter, lacemakers would set aside a small sum of money to provide cakes and tea to be enjoyed on this day. Festivities would be held in the evening, and a meal of boiled, stuffed rabbit and onions was served.

CATTERN CAKES

9 oz/275 g self-raising flour
¼ teaspoon ground cinnamon
1 oz/25 g currants
2 oz/50 g ground almonds
2 teaspoons caraway seeds
7 oz/200 g caster sugar
4 oz/100 g melted butter
1 medium egg, beaten
A little extra sugar and cinnamon for sprinkling

OVEN: 200°C/400°F/GAS 6

❖ Sift the flour and the cinnamon into a bowl and stir in the currants, almonds, caraway seeds and sugar. Add the melted butter and beaten egg and mix well to give a soft dough. Roll out on a floured board into a rectangle, about 12 × 10 inches/30 × 25 cm.

❖ Brush the dough with water and sprinkle with the extra sugar and cinnamon. Roll up like a swiss roll and cut into ¾ inch/2 cm slices. Place these slices, spaced well apart, on a greased tray and bake for 10 minutes. Cool on a wire rack. Sprinkle with extra caraway seeds if you like.

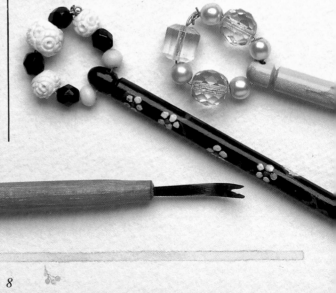

RABBIT CASSEROLE

4 rabbit joints
8 oz/225 g cooked ham (thickly sliced)
2 medium carrots, peeled
8 small shallots, peeled
1 pint/600 ml milk
½ teaspoon salt
Black pepper
¼ teaspoon grated nutmeg
Fresh parsley (optional)
½ oz/15 g cornflour
2 extra tablespoons milk
½ oz/15 g butter

OVEN: 180°C/350°F/GAS 4

❖ Wash the rabbit portions well. Pat them dry and arrange in a large, heatproof dish. Dice the ham and slice the carrots – place them, with the shallots, in the dish. Heat the milk gently and pour over the rabbit portions. Sprinkle with the salt, pepper and grated nutmeg. Add a little parsley, if liked.

❖ Cover the dish with a lid or foil and cook slowly until the rabbit is tender, about 1 hour. Transfer to a warm dish and keep warm while you make the sauce.

❖ Mix the cornflour to a smooth paste with the extra milk. Pour in the cooking liquid and stir well. Pour into a clean saucepan and cook slowly, stirring all the time, until the sauce thickens. Add the butter and simmer for 3 minutes. Pour the sauce over the rabbit portions and serve garnished with a little extra parsley.

*B*obbins were, and are, usually made of bone, wood or ivory. The set of bobbins on a lace pillow are often a personal record of the lacemaker's life, engraved perhaps with her name and the names of her loved ones, together with family births and marriages. Today bobbins can be commissioned with all sorts of inscriptions engraved, to commemorate personal and national events. The spangles used to weight the bobbins are often private mementoes – a button from a baby's shoe, a lucky charm, or a coin. Modern lacemakers buy beads and other souvenirs from outings and holidays and use these to spangle their bobbins. Thus their pillows become not just objects of beauty but a store of happy memories, priceless to each lacemaker.

Yon cottager, who weaves at her own door
Pillow and bobbins all her little store
Content, though mean, and cheerful, if not gay,
Shuffling her threads the live long day.

WILLIAM COWPER

NOVEMBER 30

St. Andrew's Day

ST. ANDREW is the fisherman apostle and is, of course, the patron saint of Scotland. There are many tales surrounding his life (and how his relics came to Scotland), and a great number of miraculous and heroic deeds were attributed posthumously to him. It is thought that a monk brought some relics to Fife in the north of Scotland, where he built (at an angel's instruction) a church in what is now the city of St. Andrew's.

When the Picts, then converted to Christianity, won a battle against the English due to 'the appearance of St. Andrew's cross in the heavens', they took the Saint as their patron. The Saint's day became a Scottish national holiday, and there is great feasting on this day.

To celebrate with the Scots, here are traditional recipes for a delicious St. Andrew's cake for tea, and roast salmi of pheasant.

ST. ANDREW'S CAKE

St. Andrew was also the patron saint of Midland lacemakers (as well as St. Catherine), and his feast day was a holiday for them.

1 lb/450 g plain flour
1 teaspoon salt
½ oz/15 g fresh or ½ tablespoon dried yeast
1 teaspoon caster sugar
½ pint/300 ml warm water
1 egg, beaten
4 oz/100 g lard, melted
4 oz/100 g currants
4 oz/100 g sugar
1 oz diced, crystallised lemon peel

OVEN: 180°C/350°F/GAS 4

❖ Sift the flour and salt into a bowl. Cream the yeast with the teaspoon of sugar and blend in the water. Leave the yeast to froth and bubble, then mix with the beaten egg and add to the flour. Pour in the cooled, melted lard and mix until smooth. Knead well, cover and leave to double in size.

❖ Knock back the dough and knead in the currants, sugar, and peel. Transfer to a greased 2 lb/1 kg loaf tin. Leave to rise until the dough reaches the top of the tin, 20–30 minutes, and then bake for 60–70 minutes until well risen and golden. Cool on a wire rack. Slice and serve with butter.

SALMI OF PHEASANT

1 young pheasant, roasted
FOR THE SAUCE
1 oz/25 g butter
1 teaspoon olive oil
1 oz/25 g chopped lean bacon
½ small onion, finely chopped
½ small stick celery, finely chopped
7 oz/200 g mushrooms, finely chopped
1 small carrot, finely chopped
1 oz/25 g plain flour
¾ pint/450 ml hot beef stock
2 teaspoons tomato purée
1 bay leaf
2 sprigs parsley
Salt and pepper
3–4 tablespoons port
1 tablespoon redcurrant jelly

OVEN: 200°C/400°F/GAS 6

❖ Joint the pheasant, remove the skin and put medium-sized pieces into a large heatproof dish.
❖ Make up the sauce by heating the butter and the oil in a pan until bubbling. Add the bacon, onion, celery, 1 oz/25 g of the mushrooms and carrot, and sauté gently for 10 minutes.
❖ Stir in the flour and cook until it turns light brown. Gradually blend in the beef stock and stir until the sauce comes to the boil and starts to thicken. Add the tomato purée, bay leaf and parsley. Simmer gently for 30 minutes.
❖ Strain the sauce and season to taste. Stir in the port and redcurrant jelly. Add the remaining 6 oz/175 g mushrooms, then pour the sauce over the jointed grouse and simmer for 10 minutes.

One of the most beautiful of Scottish crafts was that of Ayrshire flowerin' or Scottish sewed muslin. Fine white embroidery on sheer muslin, it was designed to be seen against the skin and is thought to be some of the most skilled needlework in the world. Legend has it that St. Mungo travelled through Northern Ireland and Scotland preaching the gospel. During his travels he found a baby lying in the back of a cave, dressed in a fine, white robe, so finely wrought that no human could have made it. This story became the inspiration for needleworkers and Christening robes and bonnets were made in this beautiful manner.

December

Advent Sunday

THIS ALWAYS FALLS on the nearest Sunday to St. Andrew's Day. Advent signifies the arrival of the Messiah, and the period of Advent must contain the four Sundays before Christmas.

The Christian church year begins on Advent Sunday, but the origins of the festival are much older, in the ancient rituals of fire and light held during the winter solstice – perhaps reflected in our present-day Advent candles.

The Advent ring is traditionally hung up in homes today, the start of the Advent season. It contains four candles, one to be lit for a while on Advent Sunday, one to be lit the next Sunday and so on until four are lit. These four candles are then lit together on Christmas Eve to welcome the Christ-child. Advent calendars are also a popular tradition, originally from Germany, with little 'windows' to be opened daily, finishing on Christmas Eve.

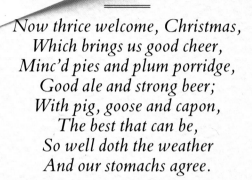

Now thrice welcome, Christmas,
Which brings us good cheer,
Minc'd pies and plum porridge,
Good ale and strong beer;
With pig, goose and capon,
The best that can be,
So well doth the weather
And our stomachs agree.

NOW THRICE WELCOME CHRISTMAS
ANON

MINCEMEAT

The mincemeat of early years was minced meat – beef or tongue being most commonly used. Up to the seventeeth century, mince pie was in fact called Christmas pie, and was made in one huge dish, filled with ox tongue, chicken, eggs, raisins, candied peel, sugar and spices. It was common practice in those days (in fact ever since the Crusaders) to combine sweet and savoury ingredients in one dish – although there is also a theory that the meat was originally mixed with fruit in this manner to disguise it from the prying eyes of more zealous Christians during holy periods (such as Lent), when the eating of meat was forbidden.

8 oz/225 g cooking apples
8 oz/225 g currants
8 oz/225 g sultanas
4 oz/100 g glacé cherries
4 oz/100 g dates
4 oz/100 g crystallized peel
4 oz/100 g chopped walnuts
8 oz/225 g unsalted butter, softened
1 lb/450 g demerara sugar
2 teaspoons ground mixed spice
4 fl oz/125 ml brandy, rum or Grand Marnier

❖ Peel, core and dice the apples. Mince, with all the dried fruit and walnuts, and mix in a large bowl with the butter, sugar and mixed spice. Stir in the brandy, rum or Grand Marnier. Mix well and put into clean, dry jars, and cover as for jam. This is a relatively short-term preserve, but should keep for up to three months – though I have never managed to last out that long!

❖ Cooks sometimes used to add a pinch of powdered rosemary to their mincemeat in honour of Mary. Legend says that as she fled with her baby into Egypt a rosemary bush held out its branches for her to dry the baby's clothes on.

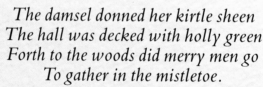

DECEMBER 21

St. Thomas' Day

ST. THOMAS' DAY, or Thomasmas, falls on the 21st December, very near the true solstice – the turning point of the year, with the longest night and the shortest day. Its importance in the Christian calendar stems from ancient rituals surrounding the solstice, as of course do many Christmas celebrations.

For many people St. Thomas' Day was an excuse for 'gooding' – a custom of begging for Christmas food in return for little presents, often of evergreen. This was also called 'doleing', and St. Thomas' Dole often consisted of some flour to make bread for Christmas. Often a wealthy farmer would donate a bag of grain, which the local miller would grind for no charge and distribute to the poor.

For some St. Thomas' Eve (the 20th) was considered to be very holy, and no work was done at all. Young unmarried girls in many areas used to place a sprig of evergreen under their pillows when they went to bed on this night, in the expectation of dreaming of their future husbands. Evergreens were extremely significant in pagan times, symbolising the perennial fertility of Nature – they were often used for divination at the time of the solstice.

A quaint gardening tradition is still continued in many areas, in which broad beans are always planted on St. Thomas' Day. (In the South-west of England this is done instead on Guy Fawkes night.) Beans were considered to have supernatural significance, and linked sometimes with doom – if one bean in the row came up white, a death in the family would be feared.

The damsel donned her kirtle sheen
The hall was decked with holly green
Forth to the woods did merry men go
To gather in the mistletoe.

SIR WALTER SCOTT
MARMION

St. Thomas gray, St. Thomas gray
Longest night, and shortest day.

TRADITIONAL

DECEMBER 24

Christmas Eve

THE CHRISTMAS PERIOD (which officially stretches from 25th December to 6th January, or Twelfth Night) begins properly for many people on Christmas Eve, though preparations have usually been made long before that!

Father Christmas has been a traditional figure in England in some form since at least the 15th century, although the character we know now is mainly influenced by America's Santa Claus (who is based on the 4th-century Dutch St. Nicolas). Riding in a reindeer-drawn sleigh, Father Christmas comes in the dead of night on Christmas Eve, climbing down every chimney to fill stockings with presents. Often a glass of sherry and a mince pie are left out for him which, as proof that he exists, have mysteriously vanished in the morning.

Midnight Mass on Christmas Eve is heralded by the pealing of Christmas bells – at All Saint's Church in Dewsbury, West Yorkshire, there is a special bell-ringing known as 'tolling the Devil's knell'. A famous bell, called 'Black Tom of Southill' is struck once for every year since Christ was born, finishing exactly at midnight. One extra ring is then struck to ensure that the Devil is vanquished for another year.

This is a very religious night, and there used to be many stories of country folk who saw their cattle kneeling in their stables – even uttering words! Another, very sweet, belief in some places is that bees in their hives will hum the hundredth Psalm on Christmas Eve.

Christmas Eve was traditionally the time to bring in the Christmas decorations – nowadays these are often put up before, but it is still considered un-lucky by some to put up evergreens before 24th December. Holly, ivy and mistletoe are popularly used. Mistletoe was considered a potent symbol of male virility, and this notion has continued in the form of our present custom of kissing under the mistletoe – traditionally, a male can use the plant to assert his supremacy in an age-old right of demanding a kiss; some say one kiss for each berry. Of course, as many women as men now take advantage of the mistletoe!

Before the introduction of the Christmas tree, the main decoration of the home used to be the kissing bough – a ball or circle of evergreens, adorned with ribbons and fruit, from which hung mistletoe and small presents. This would be a lovely idea to copy.

Christmas Eve was, traditionally, the time for the Mummers to come to enact their plays. Mummers are usually disguised (they are called 'guisers' in many parts of northern England and Scotland), and used to perform in mime, although speech is now used. The Mummers would often enact a play based on the story of St. George and the Dragon. They would perform their little tale in the houses of all the most important people of the village. The Company, made up of young men, would depict a range of traditional characters and each make an appropriate speech. 'Old Father Christmas' would carry a holly bough and wassail bowl, and 'The Pretty Girl' would have a sprig of mistletoe. Then would come the enemy, 'The Grand Turk' (sometimes called 'Bold Slasher') and then the gallant knight 'St. George'. A 'Doctor' is on hand to revive the slain hero, and finally, to frighten the children, there would be a fearful 'Dragon'. The form of all Mummers' plays are usually much the same, although the names of characters and topical allusions may vary.

At Christmas I no more desire a rose
Than wish a snow in May's new-fangled
mirth,
But like of each thing that in season
grows.

WILLIAM SHAKESPEARE
LOVE'S LABOUR'S LOST

CRYSTALLISED PEEL

Making your own peel makes such a difference to the finished taste of your Christmas fare, it is well worth the extra trouble involved.

3 oranges
2 lemons
½ oz/15 g bicarbonate of soda
1½ lb/750 g granulated sugar

❖ Wash the fruit well, and cut the oranges into large halves crossways and the lemons into halves lengthways. Scoop out all the pulp and put the peel into a large earthenware, glass or plastic bowl. Dissolve the bicarbonate of soda in ¼ pint/150 ml of hot water and pour over the peel. Leave to soak for 30 minutes and then drain and wash well.

❖ Put the peel into a saucepan and cover with cold water. Bring to the boil and simmer until tender. In a separate pan boil 1 lb/450 g of the sugar with ¾ pint/450 ml of water to make a syrup. Drain the peel well and put back into the earthenware bowl, then pour over the sugar syrup. Cover with a clean tea towel and leave to stand for two days.

❖ Strain the syrup back into the pan, add the rest of the sugar and boil. Add the peel and simmer until it becomes transparent. Lift out the peel with a slotted spoon and put on a baking sheet. Dry in a slow oven. 110°C/225°F/Gas ¼.

❖ Boil up the sugar syrup again and dip in the peel, then return the peel to the oven to dry again. Simmer the rest of the syrup until it becomes thick and cloudy. Pour a little into each dried peel cap and leave to dry completely. Store in an airtight container until ready to use. Peel keeps best when made in large pieces, as here, and should only be chopped when ready to use.

What will go into the Christmas Stocking,
While the clock on the mantlepiece is ticking.
An orange, a penny,
Some sweets, not too many.
A handful of love,
Another of fun,
And it's very nearly done.

ELEANOR FARJEON
CHRISTMAS STOCKING

THE YULE LOG

*T*he tradition of burning a yule log on Christmas Eve is an ancient one – a large forest log, found or given but not bought, would be brought with great ceremony into the Manor House on this evening. Songs were sung in its honour and guests had to pay tribute before passing on. It was thought that as the log burned it would burn away all bad luck and old wrong. A small piece of one year's log would be kept to light the next year's yule log.

As the tradition of burning the yule log has died, we can keep the custom alive by baking a chocolate yule log to eat on Christmas Day.

3 medium eggs
3 oz/75 g caster sugar, plus extra for sprinkling
Few drops vanilla essence
1 oz/25 g drinking chocolate
3 oz/75 g plain flour, sifted
FOR DECORATION
8 oz/225 g vanilla buttercream
8 oz/225 g chocolate buttercream
2–4 oz/50–100 g almond paste (see page 53)
3 oz/75 g chocolate glacé icing
Icing sugar, for sifting

OVEN: 200°C/400°F/GAS 6

❖ Grease and line a swiss roll tin. Whisk the eggs, sugar and vanilla essence together in a bowl placed over a pan of hot water or in an electric mixer, until the mixture resembles lightly whipped cream. Remove from the heat and continue beating until cool. Fold in the drinking chocolate and sifted flour very carefully with a metal spoon. Try not to beat too much air from the mixture.

❖ Spoon the mixture on to the baking tin. Do not spread it, but tilt the tin around until the mixture covers the tin evenly. Bake for 12–14 minutes or until springy to the touch and shrunken from the sides. Turn the cake out on to a sheet of sugared greaseproof paper which has been placed on top of a damp tea towel. Gently peel off the greaseproof paper and roll up the swiss roll.

❖ Leave to cool and then unroll gently. Remove the damp towel and greaseproof paper. Spread over the vanilla buttercream, leaving a small margin around the edges, and roll up carefully.

❖ Roll out two circles of almond paste to fit the ends of the log, put a little buttercream on one side, and push into place. Cover the log with chocolate buttercream and mark the surface with a fork to resemble bark. Pipe rings on the marzipan with chocolate glacé icing to make the rings in the log. Decorate the log with mushrooms shaped from almond paste and dredge with icing sugar.

DECEMBER 25

Christmas Day

LATE DECEMBER has always been a time of low spirits – everything appears to be at a low ebb and the time of renewal is still far away. From the time of earliest man therefore, this period was chosen as a time for celebrating and looking forward to better days to come. Our present-day festival celebrating the birth of Christ is rooted in many pre-Christian traditions around the time of the winter solstice.

In northern Europe Odin was worshipped with festivals of eating and drinking; the Yule Feast of the Norsemen. Log fires were burned to aid the ailing sun and sacred places were decked with ivy and bay. In the 4th century the Roman emperor Constantine was converted to Christianity, and he decided to substitute Christian festivals for the pagan ones rather than trying to ban the latter altogether. The British took to the new celebration and slowly abandoned the druid rites they had clung to.

Feasting on the 25th December has continued to this day, although in Puritan times all such 'heathen' celebration was banned – in 1644 the Parliament, incensed by the lack of religion and general uproar surrounding the festival, declared that the holiness of 25th December should be marked by fasting, and troops toured the streets of London to make sure there were no dinners cooking on this day. However, with the restoration of the monarchy and the return of Charles II, England again began to celebrate Christmas as a time of great jollity.

In the last century a more personal, family-based Christmas became popular. Prince Albert brought his German Christmas traditions to England, and Charles Dickens wrote about Christmas as a time of peace and goodwill to all men in 'A Christmas Carol'. It is felt by many – myself included – that our modern Christmas has become a great deal too commercialised, and that it may be time to return to a more personal occasion as it was in Victorian times.

Christmas dinner is now traditionally roast turkey and Christmas pudding, but before turkey became popular a boar's head was the centrepiece (and is in fact still served today at Queen's College, Oxford). Goose, roast beef and chicken were also popular in more recent times.

ROAST TURKEY

10 lb/5 kg turkey
Lemon juice
2–3 slices of stale bread, fried in butter
Large pinch of mixed herbs/ Salt and pepper
Port and fruit stuffing (see opposite)
8 oz/225 g butter, melted
Few rashers fat bacon
Good giblet stock

OVEN: 200°C/400°F/GAS 6

❖ Wipe the turkey, inside and out, with a damp cloth and pat dry. Remove any feathers and the fat sac from the tail. Rub the tail well with salt and lemon juice. Fill the cavity of the turkey with the fried bread and season well with the herbs, salt and pepper. Calculate cooking time: 20 minutes per pound/450 g, plus 20 minutes over.

❖ Loosen the skin around the breast of the turkey by running your hand between the skin and the flesh. Push the stuffing into this pocket on both sides of the breast bone. Be careful not to pack too tightly, as the skin will burst when the stuffing expands during cooking. Truss the turkey, put it into a large roasting pan and season well with salt and black pepper. Prick the breast of the bird with a sharp skewer and rub with some of the melted butter. Lay over a few rashers of fat bacon.

❖ Roast the turkey on the lowest shelf of the oven for 15 minutes. Baste well with melted butter and reduce the heat to 180°C/350°F/Gas 4. Roast for a further 15 minutes, turn the turkey over, baste again and cook for another 15 minutes. Turn the turkey on to its back again, replace the bacon rashers and baste well. (It is necessary to baste the bird well to keep the flesh moist.) Roast for the remainder of the cooking time, continuing to baste.

❖ To test that the turkey is cooked, move the thigh in its socket. It should move freely. If in any doubt, check by running a skewer into the thickest part of the thigh. The juices should run clear, with no pink.

CHESTNUT STUFFING

8 oz/225 g chestnuts
4 oz/100 g white breadcrumbs
2 teaspoons finely grated onion
½ teaspoon salt
¼ teaspoon nutmeg
Black pepper
2 oz/50 g melted butter
Single cream

❖ Boil chestnuts in water for 30 minutes. Drain and leave to cool, then shell them and pass through a fine sieve. Combine with breadcrumbs, onion, salt and nutmeg. Season well with black pepper. Bind with melted butter and single cream.

CHRISTMAS PUDDING

IN DAYS GONE BY, plum pottage (the fore-runner of our Christmas pudding) was served as a first course. It was then made with a little meat, spiced with cloves and ginger and made to go further with the addition of breadcrumbs, raisins and prunes. Plum pudding, now with sugar and no beef, has become the traditional end to the Christmas meal.

The recipe for Christmas pudding will be found in the November chapter under 'Stir-Up Sunday' (see page 120) and, if made then, will have matured nicely by now.

On Christmas morning, re-cover the pudding with fresh greaseproof paper and a clean cloth. Steam steadily for 2–3 hours or pressure-cook for 40 minutes. When ready to serve, put on to a warm serving dish. Pour over warmed brandy and add a sprig of holly. Light the brandy and carry the pudding triumphantly to the table. Serve with Cumberland rum butter.

Observe how the chimneys
Do smoke all about,
The cooks are providing
For dinner, no doubt.
For those on whose tables
No victuals appear,
O may they keep Lent
All the rest of the year!

NOW THRICE WELCOME CHRISTMAS
ANON

CUMBERLAND RUM BUTTER

8 oz/225 g unsalted butter, softened
12 oz/350 g soft brown sugar
4 fl oz/125 ml rum
Ground cinnamon
Toasted almonds

❖ Beat the butter in a bowl until soft and creamy. Beat in the sugar until thoroughly blended. Gradually add the rum, beating well after each addition. Add cinnamon to taste and chill well before serving. Store in small jars.

❖ This butter will keep well in the refrigerator for several weeks. When ready to serve pile the butter into a pretty dish and sprinkle with toasted almonds and extra cinnamon.

MINCE PIES

The secret of successful shortcrust pastry is the type of fat you use – a solid block margarine, one intended specifically for baking, has a high melting temperature and ensures a light texture. This will make enough for about 12 mince pies.

FOR THE PASTRY
8 oz/225 g plain flour
¼ teaspoon salt
4 oz/100 g margarine
4–5 tablespoons iced water, to mix

FOR THE FILLING
8 oz/225 g mincemeat
1 tablespoon brandy (optional)
1 egg, beaten, to glaze
Icing sugar, sifted

OVEN: 220°C/425°F/GAS 7

❖ Sift the flour and salt into a bowl. Cut the margarine into the flour with a round-bladed knife. Rub in quickly with the fingertips. Sprinkle on the water and knead until smooth. Leave to rest in the refrigerator, wrapped in greaseproof paper and a polythene bag or cling film for 30 minutes. Knead again lightly to soften before rolling out two thirds to line the greased bun tins.

❖ If you use a processor to make your pastry, remember to stop as soon as the mixture starts to form a ball. If you overmix your pastry will be like leather.

❖ Stir a tablespoon of brandy into the mincemeat if you like, then spoon into the pastry cases. Roll out the remaining pastry to make the lids, place them on the cases and brush with beaten egg. Bake in the centre of the oven for 20–25 minutes. Remove from the tins, cool and dredge with sifted icing sugar.

❖ For an extra treat, use a knife to lift the lid gently off the mince pies and add a teaspoon of Cumberland rum butter before replacing the lid.

The traditional Christmas toast used to be 'waes hael', Anglo Saxon for 'to your health'. A wassail bowl, often made from ash or maple, would be filled with ale and decorated with ribbons or holly and ivy. This bowl was passed around for the drinking of mutual healths, and wassailers took the bowl from door to door through the village – often the wassailers were poorer villagers, and they took the bowl to their more prosperous neighbours in the hope that gifts of money would be made in exchange for the Christmas goodwill toast. This delightful custom was once practised all over England during the Christmas and New Year period, but has now virtually died out. Grampound in Cornwall is one village where wassailing still occurs.

LAMB'S WOOL

In Yorkshire the wassail toast would be 'to wool and mutton', the staples of the prosperous Dales farmers. This drink is called lamb's wool as the apple pulp could fancifully be likened to wool.

6 pints/2.8 litres brown ale
1½ pints/750 ml sweet white wine
½ nutmeg, grated
1 teaspoon ground ginger
1 stick cinnamon
4–5 baked apples
Brown sugar, to taste

❖ Heat the ale, wine and spices together in a large pan. Skin the apples and mash them to a pulp. Pour over the liquid, having first removed the cinnamon. Mix together and strain through a cloth. Add sugar to taste and reheat. Drink hot.

And is it true? And is it true,
This most tremendous tale of all,
Seen in a stained-glass window's hue,
A baby in an ox's stall?

SIR JOHN BETJEMAN
CHRISTMAS

DECEMBER 26

Boxing Day

BOXING DAY was the day chosen by employers to give their servants or staff small gifts of money – this custom still survives when the local postmen and dustmen call to wish us 'compliments of the season' in exchange for a small Christmas 'box'. This day, 26th December, is also St. Stephen's day, commemorating the first male Christian martyr who was stoned to death in Jerusalem in 33 A.D. He was one of our most popular saints in the Middle Ages, but is now largely forgotten, except in the carol 'Good King Wenceslas'.

Boxing Day had until recently been the day for hunting wrens, squirrels and other small animals. 'The Hunting of the Wren' was a rather sinister custom extremely popular in Wales, south-western England, southern Ireland and the Isle of Man. A wren was hunted and killed, hung on a pole and processed through the town – donations were collected 'on behalf of the wren' in exchange for its feathers, which were considered lucky. In some areas the wren was carried in a garland of decorated bush of holly or gorse – in Kerry, Ireland, the bird was put live into a glass jar. Of course nowadays the wren is no longer hunted, and the bush does not contain anything (and there have been cases of potatoes being carried in the jar!).

Whatever way you choose to spend Boxing Day, you will doubtless have lots of Christmas pudding from yesterday to use up, and this is a good way to transform it.

DEVONSHIRE RUM PUDDING

Cold Christmas pudding, cut into fingers
1 rounded tablespoon cornflour
1 pint/600 ml milk
1 tablespoon caster sugar
1 egg, beaten
3 fl oz/75 ml rum, more if liked
Grated nutmeg

OVEN: 190°C/375°F/GAS 5

❖ Butter a 2 pint/1.5 litre pie dish and arrange the Christmas pudding fingers in the base. Sprinkle with a few tablespoons of rum if you like. Mix the cornflour to a smooth paste with a little of the milk, heat the rest of the milk and add the blended cornflour. Cook, stirring, for 3 minutes. Off the heat, stir in the sugar, the egg and the rum. Pour the sauce over the fingers in the pie dish and sprinkle with grated nutmeg. Bake for 25–30 minutes and serve warm.

The wren, the wren, the king of all birds,
St. Stephen's Day he was caught in the furze.
Although he be little his family's great,
I pray you good lady give us a treat.

BOY'S BEGGING SONG, COUNTY KERRY

DECEMBER 31

New Year's Eve

NEW YEAR'S EVE is an increasingly popular festival in England, and has always been the most important occasion in the Scottish year. It doesn't have any Christian roots but of course has many links with old pagan celebrations of the winter solstice and the turning of the year.

Fires always used to be lit at this time all over Britain, to encourage the waning sun and as a protection against evil and witchcraft. Burning the old year out still occurs in many areas, with bonfires, flambeaux processions, swinging fireballs and even a burning viking ship in the Shetlands. A famous fire custom still celebrated today is 'Burning the Clavie' at Burghead on the Moray Firth (in fact on the *old* New Year's Eve of 11th January). A tar barrel called a clavie is set on fire and put on a 'spoke' or pole. This is then carried by relays round the village and finally rolled down a hill. Lucky brands are taken to light household fires, and embers are kept to guard against witches.

All over Britain, sirens, bells and hooters sound in the New Year at midnight, and there are toasts, kisses and singing of Auld Lang Syne. There are lots of customs about making a clean break with the past year and welcoming in the new (such as New Year resolutions!). In Scotland and North England, as the clock strikes midnight, 'first footers' are awaited with anticipation – the first person to enter the house should be a propitious one. Tall, dark, male strangers are generally considered to be the most lucky, and should always bear gifts – if they come empty-handed ill fortune will descend on the household in the coming year.

The first footers' gifts are usually coal, bread, salt and whisky – sometimes a threepenny piece, evergreen or red herrings, which symbolise plenty. In silence the head of the household should take the gifts and, in exchange, offer the stranger a glass of whisky and a piece of shortbread. This ritual ensures a happy and prosperous New Year.

The first footer is supposed to enter by the front door and leave through the back. Similarly, doors and windows are often opened on New Year's Eve, so that as the Old Year departs through the kitchen door it can take bad luck with it, and allowing the New Year and fresh hope in through the front door. In certain parts of Scotland it is also considered unlucky to have any rubbish in the house, so just before twelve, the bins are emptied – thus tipping out the bad luck of the previous year and leaving the way open for good luck to take its place.

Here is a traditional Scottish drink that is a lovely variation on the New Year whisky theme.

ATHOL BROSE

A traditional Scottish drink, this is reputed to be named after the 15th-century Earl of Athol, whose favourite tipple it was. There is a story that his enemy, the Earl of Ross, had the water in the Earl of Athol's well replaced by this drink – the Earl drank deeply and was then easily captured.

3 rounded tablespoons fine oatmeal
1 dessertspoon honey
1 fl oz/25 ml whisky

❖ Put the oatmeal in a jug and pour on enough cold water to make a thin paste. Leave to stand for a couple of minutes, then drain off the liquid and discard the oatmeal. Pour the liquid into a saucepan and heat gently. Pour into a glass and stir in the honey and whisky. Serve. It is traditional to stir this drink with a silver spoon.

Ring out wild bells to the wild sky
The flying cloud, the frosty light
The year is dying in the night
Ring out wild bells and let him die.

ALFRED LORD TENNYSON
RING OUT WILD BELLS

PETTICOAT TAILS

Traditional Scottish shortbreads, to be served to your first-footer, warm with a dram of whisky.

1 lb/450 g plain flour
8 oz/225 g butter, softened
4 oz/100 g caster sugar, plus extra for sprinkling
1 egg, beaten
Few drops of almond essence

OVEN: 110°C/220°F/GAS ½

❖ Cream all the ingredients together to form a thick paste. Roll out thinly on a floured board and, using a tea plate, cut into 4 large circles, about 7 inches/18 cm in diameter. Mark out into wedges and place on a lightly greased baking sheet. Prick over with a fork and cut out a small circle in the middle of each round to avoid the point of each biscuit breaking off when the biscuit is divided.

❖ Bake in the centre of the oven for about 1½ hours until firm and a pale golden colour. Remove from the oven and leave to cool on a rack. Sprinkle with extra caster sugar while still warm.

*I*n many parts of Wales at New Year, village men still tour their area with the Mari Lwyd or Grey Mary (or Mare). This is a horse's head, made of wood or a real skull, with coloured glass eyes and decorated with ribbons. The skull is fixed on to a pole and draped around with a sheet, and the jaw moves up and down by a handle. It is thought to be the remnants of the Celtic pagan horse worship.

The men would traditionally call at each house and challenge the occupants to a poetry contest. So long as the householder was able to cap the rhyme, then the Mari Lwyd would have to remain outside, but if they were unable to find a satisfactory reply, then they would be obliged to let the poets in and offer them refreshment. In some parts of Wales, this custom is also performed at Christmas and on Twelfth Night.

O, a ham-bone on a ceiling hook
And a goose with golden skin,
And the roaring flames of the food you cook:
For God's sake, let us in!

VERNON WATKINS
BALLAD OF THE MARI LWYD

Should auld acquaintance be forgot
And never brought to mind.
Should auld acquaintance be forgot,
For the sake of Auld Lang Syne.

ROBERT BURNS
AULD LANG SYNE

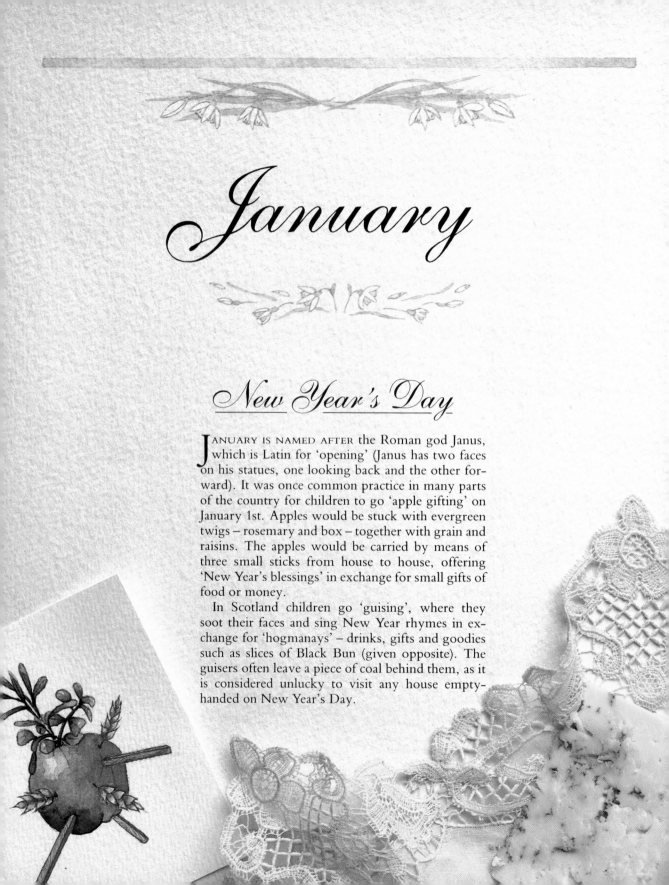

January

New Year's Day

JANUARY IS NAMED AFTER the Roman god Janus, which is Latin for 'opening' (Janus has two faces on his statues, one looking back and the other forward). It was once common practice in many parts of the country for children to go 'apple gifting' on January 1st. Apples would be stuck with evergreen twigs – rosemary and box – together with grain and raisins. The apples would be carried by means of three small sticks from house to house, offering 'New Year's blessings' in exchange for small gifts of food or money.

In Scotland children go 'guising', where they soot their faces and sing New Year rhymes in exchange for 'hogmanays' – drinks, gifts and goodies such as slices of Black Bun (given opposite). The guisers often leave a piece of coal behind them, as it is considered unlucky to visit any house empty-handed on New Year's Day.

BLACK BUN

FOR THE PASTRY
12 oz/350 g plain flour, sifted
6 oz/175 g butter
A little cold water, to mix
FOR THE FILLING
1 lb/450 g raisins
1 lb/450 g currants
3 oz/75 g almonds, blanched and chopped
4 oz/100 g crystallised peel (see page 13)
8 oz/225 g plain flour
2 oz/50 g brown sugar
1 teaspoon grated nutmeg
1 teaspoon ground ginger
Pinch of ground cloves
1 teaspoon ground cinnamon
½ teaspoon baking soda
3 eggs
1 tablespoon brandy or whisky
1–2 tablespoons milk (optional)

OVEN: 180°C/350°F/GAS 4

❖ Rub together the flour and butter in a bowl to a crumb texture and add enough cold water to make a stiff dough. Roll the pastry out thinly and use most of it to line a greased 8 inch/20 cm cake tin. Keep back enough dough to make a lid.

❖ Mix together all the dry ingredients for the filling. Beat the eggs and brandy or whisky together lightly and stir into the dry mixture to bind it. If it is too dry, add a tablespoon or two of milk. Put the fruit mixture into the tin, smooth the surface, moisten the edges of the pastry lid and cover the top. Pierce right down to the bottom of the cake in several places with a skewer and brush with a little beaten egg. Bake for about 3 hours.

POTTED STILTON

In many parts of Scotland and North England people refuse to lend anything on New Year's Day, as this is thought to bring bad luck. This recipe for using up leftovers is over 200 years old and is as good now as it was then.

8–10 oz/225–300 g Stilton crumbs
2 oz/50 g butter, softened
Pinch of mace
A little port or milk, to moisten
Clarified butter

❖ Blend the stilton, butter and mace together with enough port or milk to make a smooth, spreadable paste. Put into small ramekin dishes. Melt a little clarified butter and pour a layer over each to seal. Chill in the refrigerator until required.

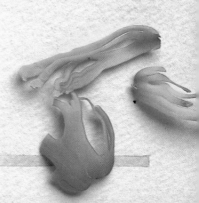

JANUARY 5

Twelfth Night

THE TWELFTH NIGHT after Christmas is a magical time, signifying the end of yule and the culmination of the Christmas jollifications. It is the time for taking down the decorations and burning the tree (it used to be thought that if you keep holly in the house after this date, each leaf and sprig of berries turns into a mischevious spirit!). Twelfth Night is a pagan festival, but was deliberately swallowed up into Epiphany by the Church in the 4th century. However, many old customs still remain.

Twelfth Night was traditionally an occasion for games, feasting and general merriment. At the royal court in Medieval times there was much revelry, forfeits, disguisings and play-acting. A Lord of Misrule, appointed at the beginning of the Christmas season, held his final court on this day. He would have led all the festivities for the last twelve days, helped by a band of twenty to forty courtiers dressed in suitably frivolous garb.

In Tudor times, a masque or play would often be presented (such as Shakespeare's 'Twelfth Night', perhaps), and the revels would be presided over by the King of the Bean or Queen of the Marrowfat (the Pea). A bean is cooked into a cake, and whoever finds it in their portion is crowned (and, in more recent versions, has to buy a round of drinks).

TWELFTH NIGHT CAKE

8 oz/225 g butter, softened
8 oz/225 g caster sugar
4 eggs, beaten
3 tablespoons brandy
8 oz/225 g plain flour
8 oz/225 g currants
8 oz/225 g raisins
8 oz/225 g sultanas
2 oz/50 g chopped nuts
Pinch of cinnamon
Dried pea or bean (optional)
TO DECORATE
Glacé cherries and crystallised fruits
Melted honey, to glaze

OVEN: 150°C/300°F/GAS 2

❖ Grease and line a 12 inch/30 cm tin. Cream the butter and sugar together and stir in the well-beaten eggs and brandy. Sift the flour and cinnamon and gradually fold into the mixture, alternately with the dried fruit and nuts. Add the pea or bean. Pour into the prepared tin and bake for 3–3¼ hours, until a skewer comes out clean. Allow the cake to cool for 15 minutes before turning out on to a wire rack.
❖ Decorate the cake with glacé cherries and crystallised fruits, and glaze with a little melted honey.

HUNTING BEEF

The following recipe has been known for some 300 years and is ideally suited to a celebration such as Twelfth Night that goes back to pre-Medieval times. There are many recipes for meats preserved in this way, which would enable meat from animals killed in October to be kept for a little while into winter.

3 lb/1.5 kg silverside of beef
2 oz/50 g cane sugar
½ oz/15 g black peppercorns
¼ oz/7 g allspice
½ oz/15 g juniper berries
1½ oz/40 g salt
¼ oz/7 g saltpetre (optional)

❖ Rub the beef with the sugar and leave for 2 days in a stoneware pot in the refrigerator.
❖ Crush all the spices with the salt and saltpetre. Rub the beef with this mixture every day for 7 days. After 7 days, remove the meat and wash well.
❖ Put the meat into an ovenproof dish and add ½ pint/300 ml water. Cover with a tight-fitting lid and bake in a slow oven, 140°C/275°F/Gas 1, for 5 hours. Remove, drain and cover with a board and weights. Refrigerate for 24 hours before carving thinly.
❖ This meat will carve well and has a lovely, spicy fragrance.

*T*here are some lovely apple orchard ceremonies that still occur at this time of year, such as Somerset apple wassailing. This is held on the old Twelfth Night (17th January), and bread soaked in cider is placed on the branches of a chosen tree while onlookers sing wassailing songs. In East Cornwall one special tree is saluted and sprinkled with cider, and in parts of West Sussex 'apple howling' takes place, where horns are blown and the trees thrashed with sticks to make them bear fruit.

Old apple tree, we wassail thee, and
hoping thou wilt bear
Hat-fulls, cap-fulls, three-bushel bagfulls
And a little heap under the stairs
Hip! Hip! Hooray!

APPLE WASSAILING SONG, NEAR MINEHEAD

JANUARY 6

Epiphany

'EPIPHANY' MEANS 'manifestation', and this festival originally celebrated the four manifestations of Christ – to the shepherds, to the wise men, at his baptism and when he changed water into wine. At first only occurring in the Eastern Orthodox Church calendar (where it is still the most important day of the year, even more than Christmas), it was adopted by the Western Church in the 4th century. This concentrated on the manifestation to the three wise men as they represented the non-Jewish Christian world. The 6th January was chosen as it coincided with (and therefore superceded) pagan celebrations of the new year.

An interesting 'Epiphany Gifts Ceremony' still takes place on 6th January at St. James' Palace in London. British monarchs used to re-enact ritually the visit of the three wise men or kings bringing gifts to the Christ-child. Since George III, this has been done by appointed representatives. Gifts of gold (in the shape of twenty-five gold sovereigns), frankincense and myrrh are placed on the altar of the Chapel Royal, and blessed by the Bishop of London.

EPIPHANY TART

Victorian housewives used to vie with each other to produce the most complicated designs, using the greatest number of different jams, and winning the competition at Church Suppers became a point of honour!

*8 oz/225 g shortcrust pastry
(see recipe on page 22)
Approx. 4 oz/100 g jam, in various types and
colours (the more the better)*

OVEN: 200°C/400°F/GAS 6

❖ Roll out the pastry and line a 9 inch/23 cm tart tin. With the pastry trimmings make a lattice pattern across the tart base. Warm the jams slightly and spread into the spaces in the lattice-work. Bake for about 25–30 minutes, until the pastry is cooked.
❖ Serve with custard or single cream.

MONDAY FOLLOWING JANUARY 5

Plough Monday

PLOUGH MONDAY falls on the first Monday after Twelfth Night. It once marked the end of the Christmas holiday period (often the only holiday of the year for farm labourers) when ploughing would begin for the next crop. In many parts of Britain it used to be a feast day.

Festive village gatherings used to occur around the country, and leaping dances were held, for which athletic young men were chosen as it was thought that the height they leaped to would be the height of the next corn harvest. In some areas farm labourers with blackened faces dragged a decorated plough (often called a 'fool plough') around the streets, and people who didn't donate would often have their garden ploughed up in retaliation. Sometimes a Fool would dance behind the plough, dressed in skins with a tail.

PLOUGHMAN'S COTTAGE LOAF

Serve this bread, still warm from the oven, with a good wedge of farmhouse cheese and a little pickle or chutney. Accompany your meal with a glass of dry cider or ale and finish with a crisp English apple, and remember the ploughmen of years ago.

1 lb/450 g strong, plain flour
2 teaspoons salt
½ oz/15 g fresh or ½ tablespoon dried yeast
½ pint/300 ml warm water

OVEN: 220°C/425°F/GAS 7

❖ Sift the flour and salt into a bowl (or a mixer bowl fitted with a dough hook, or food processor if you have one). Cream the yeast and warm water together, until the yeast has completely dissolved and is starting to froth.

❖ Tip the yeast mixture into the flour and mix until a ball of dough has formed. Stir for a further 1 minute. Cover and leave in the bowl until the dough has doubled in size. (The time this takes will depend on the warmth of the kitchen.) Knead or mix again.

❖ Divide the bread dough into one third and two thirds. Shape into two balls, one twice the size of the other, and flatten slightly. Cut a fairly deep cross in the top of the larger round and dampen slightly with water. Put the smaller round on top and, using a floured thumb or wooden spoon handle, press down through the smaller topknot and into the base.

❖ Cover with a cloth and leave to rise again for 20–30 minutes until springy to the touch. Glaze with salted water, place on a greased baking tray and bake in the oven for 30–35 minutes until hollow-sounding when tapped on the bottom.

❖ Cool on a rack.

On Plough Monday, in many areas, the ploughmen would put on their best smocks for the occasion. Smock frocks for labourers were at the height of their popularity in the 18th century. Smock is an old English word for a shift or chemise – it was the everyday wear of shepherds and drovers, but general labourers would keep their smocks to wear for special occasions and for hiring fairs. Old smocking patterns include tree symbols for foresters, wheels for carters and rams' horns for shepherds. The heavy linen originally used for smocks was quite waterproof and windproof and would offer considerable protection to the wearer, even in wintertime.

Turn out for Plow Monday
Up, fellows, now
Buckle the horses
And follow the plough.

OXFORDSHIRE PLOUGHBOYS' CHANT

SHEPHERD'S PIE

A popular dish associated with farm workers of long ago is Shepherd's Pie, and this recipe is a modern interpretation.

12 oz/350 g cold, cooked mutton or lamb
FOR THE GOOD, BROWN SAUCE
1 oz/25 g butter
1 oz/25 g chopped bacon
1/2 small onion, peeled and diced
1/2 stick celery, diced
1 oz/25 g mushrooms, sliced
1/2 small carrot, peeled and diced
1 oz/25 g flour
3/4 pint/450 ml brown stock or water
1 small tomato, peeled and de-seeded
1 bay leaf
Bunch of sweet herbs
Salt and black pepper
FOR THE TOPPING
1 lb/450 g potatoes, mashed
1 egg yolk
A little single cream
2–4 oz/50–100 g cheese, grated

OVEN: 220°C/425°F/GAS 7

❖ Mince the mutton or lamb and place in a large pie dish. Make the sauce: put the butter into a pan, heat and add the bacon, onion, celery, mushrooms and carrot. Fry gently until golden brown. Add the flour and cook, stirring all the time, until the flour turns a rich golden brown. Blend in the stock or water and cook, stirring, until the mixture thickens. Add the tomato, bay leaf and herbs. Cover and simmer for 40 minutes. Strain, adjust the seasoning and pour the sauce over the meat. Stir well.
❖ Top the dish with the mashed potatoes, to which an egg yolk and cream have been added. Sprinkle with the grated cheese and cook in the oven for 20 minutes until golden brown and bubbling.

JANUARY 20

St. Agnes' Eve

ST. AGNES WAS martyred in Rome under the Emperor Diocletian. Because she refused to marry and deny her faith, she was stripped and sent to a brothel as a punishment. According to legend her hair suddenly grew miraculously to cover her, and an angel brought her a white robe.

It is traditionally believed that on St. Agnes' Eve girls will dream of their future partners – strange perhaps for a saint who symbolises chastity! If you are single and would like to dream of your future love, follow this simple procedure, which has been practised for many centuries: with your wish in mind, pick pins from a pincushion (some people say you must recite a Pater Noster, too) and stick them in your sleeve. When you go to bed, be sure to lie on your back with your hands behind your head. Having accomplished all this, you will dream of a kiss in the night . . .

Perhaps, then, an early night is called for on St. Agnes' Eve? Here is a very old recipe for a soothing dish with which to retire, a posset (or 'ducks' if you live in the Midlands).

POSSET

2 medium slices stale bread
Pinch of salt
Pinch of grated nutmeg
1 dessertspoon caster sugar
1 pint/600 ml milk
1 tablespoon brandy or sweet sherry

❖ Take the crusts off the bread and discard. Cut the bread into small squares. Put into a bowl and sprinkle with a pinch of salt, a pinch of nutmeg and the sugar. Bring the milk nearly to the boil, then pour it over the bread. Cover and leave to stand for 10 minutes. Stir in the brandy or sherry and serve.

They told her how, upon St. Agnes Eve
Young virgins might have visions of delight
And soft adorings from their loves receive
Upon the honey'd middle of the night.

JOHN KEATS
THE EVE OF ST. AGNES

In winter, the lacemaker, working in fine white thread, would find some difficulty in keeping her work clean. A fire was often not feasible in cold weather, because of the dust and ashes which would affect the colour of the lace. A 'dicky pot' would then be employed. It was a pot filled with hot ashes and placed under a footstool at the lacemaker's feet. With her skirts spread over this, it would keep her lower limbs warm, at least.

JANUARY 25

Burns' Night

SCOTLAND'S GREATEST POET, Robert Burns (1759–1796) is remembered every year on this night. He is celebrated by a special Burns' Night Supper, which involves much merrymaking, drinking of toasts and the eating of haggis. The meal is rounded off by speeches and recitations of Burns' narrative poems the most popular of which is usually 'Tam O'Shanter'. Often the evening is concluded by communal singing of 'Auld Lang Syne'.

Haggis, the indispensable dish for Burns' Night, is made from a sheep's stomach stuffed with the heart, lungs and liver of the animal, and oatmeal. The best haggis has venison liver instead of sheep's liver, as this gives a more robust flavour. The most commonly used recipe for haggis is based upon an old 1787 recipe by a Mrs MacIver, who lived in Edinburgh.

Here, then, are recipes for Scotch Broth and Haggis, for your own Burns' Night Supper . . .

SCOTCH BROTH

1 lb/450 g neck of mutton
4 pints/2.5 litres brown stock
3 teaspoons salt
Bunch of herbs
1 oz/25 g pearl barley
2 carrots, peeled and diced
1 medium onion, finely chopped
1 leek, trimmed and very finely sliced
2 oz/50 g peas
2 oz/50 g white cabbage, shredded

❖ Trim the fat off the mutton and place the meat in a saucepan. Add the stock, salt and herbs. Rinse the barley well and add that to the pan. Bring to the boil, skimming well, then cover and simmer gently for 1 hour.

❖ Add the carrot, onion and leek to the pan and simmer gently for 25 minutes. Finally, add the peas and cabbage and cook for a further 10 minutes. Remove the meat, leave to cool slightly and remove any excess fat and bones. Chop up the meat and return it to the pan. Adjust the seasoning and reheat.

HAGGIS

The haggis is usually brought ceremoniously to the table to the accompaniment of a piper, and placed before the chief guest. Serve the haggis traditionally by first cutting a St. Andrew's-shaped cross in the top and then opening up the pudding by folding back the flaps. Allow a dram of whisky for each guest to drink as a toast to the haggis.

1 sheep's paunch (stomach) or synthetic boiling bag
Sheep's pluck (heart, lungs and liver)
4 oz/100 g grated suet
1 large onion, chopped
1 lb/450 g pinhead oatmeal, toasted
8 oz/225 g blanched chopped almonds
1 oz/25 g salt
Black pepper
Cayenne pepper
½ teaspoon mixed herbs
Juice and grated rind of 1 lemon

❖ If using a sheep's paunch, wash it well in cold water, and scrape and clean thoroughly. Leave overnight in cold water. Also the night before, wash the sheep's pluck, put into a pan of boiling water and boil for 2 hours, with the windpipe hanging out of the pan (have a small bowl beneath it to catch any drips). Leave the pluck in the cooking liquid overnight.

❖ Next day, cut off the windpipe, and mince the liver, heart and lungs. Mix with the grated suet and onion, the lightly toasted oatmeal and the finely chopped almonds. Add the salt, pepper, cayenne pepper, herbs, lemon juice and rind. Blend in the strained liquid in which the pluck was cooked. Mix thoroughly and fill the sheep's paunch just over half full. Sew up the paunch and prick with a fork. If using a synthetic bag, tie firmly, but do not prick. Place the haggis in boiling water and simmer for 3 hours, pricking occasionally to prevent bursting.

To a haggis
Fair fa' your honest sonsie face
Great chieftain o' the puddin' race!

ROBERT BURNS

Closely associated with Scotland, and the Stuart period, is Jacobean embroidery. This is distinguished by its formalised representations of flowers and leaves. Originally worked in bright, crewel wools, it has now become associated with muted, dusky colours – the colours of the originals having faded over the years. Jacobean embroidery was used to decorate (and make more homely) the cold, draughty castles and great houses of the period, and is found on cushions, tapestries and bed hangings.

Lang may your lum reek.
(Long may your chimney smoke.)

SCOTTISH TOAST

February

Candlemas

CANDLEMAS IS THE POPULAR NAME for the feast of the Purification of St. Mary the Virgin and the Presentation of Christ in the Temple. When Mary presented Jesus at the Temple, Simeon said that Christ would be 'a light to lighten world'. Up to the time of the Reformation in England, lights were used on Candlemas day to symbolise Christ as the Light of the World. Candles were first blessed by the clergy and then given to the people to be carried in procession through the church. Every window of the church and in homes would be illuminated with a candle, if possible. If there were not enough candles available, just the kitchen window would be lit.

February 2nd was chosen by the Catholic Church for Candlemas Day as it coincided with the ancient Celtic feast of Imbolc, which came at the beginning of the lambing season and was presided over by the Celtic goddess of youth and fertility, Bride. The fires and lights of Imbolc were translated into symbols of the Purification of Mary, and Bride was re-named St. Bridget. Often called the 'Virgin

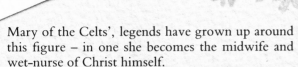

Mary of the Celts', legends have grown up around this figure – in one she becomes the midwife and wet-nurse of Christ himself.

Church candlelight rituals were frowned on after the Reformation as Popish and superstitious, but they have never been entirely extinguished. Candles are still blessed in church in many places for use in the coming year, and tapers are lit in honour of Jesus and the Virgin Mary. Snowdrops, a symbol of purity, are also called Candlemas bells or Mary's tapers, and they used to be dedicated to the Virgin on this day. There is a quaint custom in Blidworth, Nottinghamshire, where the most newly baptized baby boy of the parish is presented to the vicar on the Sunday nearest to Candlemas, and rocked in a cradle throughout the service.

A number of customs relating to pre-Christian beliefs were practised in Britain until quite recently. In Ireland a traditional St. Brigid's Eve Supper would be held, consisting of tea and boxty. The day was spent in cleaning and even painting the house and the table would be laid with the best tea things. Before the meal St. Bridget, represented again by a sheaf of straw wrapped in a garment, would be welcomed into the house. The sheaf would be placed on a chair near to the table while the meal was eaten.

BOXTY

This is an adaptation of the original potato cake dish. It will make about 6–8 cakes.

2 oz/50 g bacon fat or dripping
8 oz/225 g plain flour
½ teaspoon bicarbonate of soda
8 oz/225 g potatoes, boiled and mashed
2 oz/50 g cheese, finely grated
2 fl oz/50 ml buttermilk
1 tablespoon chopped fresh parsley
Salt and black pepper

OVEN: 200°C/400°F/GAS 6

❖ Melt the bacon fat or dripping in a pan and stir in the flour and bicarbonate of soda. Add the mashed potatoes and cheese, and mix well, then add the buttermilk, parsley and seasoning and stir to a fairly soft dough.
❖ Roll out the dough on a floured surface to about ½ inch/1 cm thick and then cut into rounds with 3 inch/7.5 cm cutter. Place on a greased baking sheet and cook for 15–20 minutes until well risen and golden. Split open and serve with plenty of butter.

If Candlemas Day be fair and bright
Winter will take another flight.
If Candlemas Day be cloud and rain
Winter is gone and will not come again.

TRADITIONAL

FEBRUARY 14

Valentine's Day

LEGEND POPULARLY HAS IT (though there is no real evidence to substantiate this) that St. Valentine's Day originated in the Roman feasts of Lupercalia, which occurred at this time of year, and the martyrdom of a certain Saint Valentine. In fact there were two Saint Valentines martyred in Rome in 269–270 A.D., about the same time as the Lupercalian festival, who have generally become confused – one was the Bishop of Terni, the other a priest or physician who is also often invoked by sufferers of epilepsy.

The Roman Lupercalian fertility rites in mid-February were held in honour of the Goddess Februata Juno (or, according to some, Pan). On that day boys would draw by lot names of unmarried girls for courtship. The 14th February was probably also chosen for St. Valentine's Day because, in folklore, it is the day on which birds choose their mates. The two bluebirds which figure on so many Valentine cards therefore represent two lovers bound together in spirit from this day on – a pretty conceit.

A Victorian game popular on St. Valentine's Day, which recalls the Roman custom of drawing lots, is still played in parts of Britain today. For this game, an equal number of girls and boys would write their names on scraps of paper, which were then put into two bowls. They then took turns to draw a name from the dish. Thus each player received two Valentines, one they themselves had drawn and one who had drawn their name. Discrimination arose, however, in that the man stayed with the girl he had chosen, and rejected the girl who had chosen him. Thus paired, the party would begin, and each couple would remain together at least until the end of the day.

Valentine's Day is for sending cards, love messages, poems and romantic presents. The idea of sending sentimental cards to loved ones is a Victorian one, and they developed it into a fine art, with ornate cards decorated with real flowers, lace, bird feathers and even hearts of spun glass. Cards declined in popularity for a while (perhaps because the taste for coarse, lewd cards became as pronounced in late Victorian times as it often seems today), but they are now enjoying a revival.

In the 18th century, lovers in the Lyme Regis area would have their initials entwined and worked together into a piece of lace. Lyme Regis lace was of very fine quality and would have been quite slow to work. How many romances were finished before the lace was, I wonder?

If you have someone to whom you would pledge your heart, why not make a heart-shaped Valentine's cake, or, if you have not yet made up your mind, bake a batch of Valentine buns or biscuits, each iced with the name of a suitor. Failing that, children (and adults) would love some heart-shaped biscuits for tea, iced with their own names or love-heart mottos, such as 'Kiss Me Quick' or 'Be Mine'.

VALENTINE BUNS (PLUM SHUTTLES)

These buns are shaped like weavers' shuttles and were once traditional on this day.

1 lb/450 g plain flour
½ teaspoon salt
½ oz/15 g fresh or ½ tablespoon dried yeast
½ tablespoon sugar
2 fl oz/50 ml warm water
2 oz/50 g butter
4 fl oz/125 ml warm milk
1 egg
8 oz/225 g currants

OVEN: 200°C/400°F/GAS 6

❖ Sift the flour and salt into a bowl. Cream the yeast and sugar together and mix with the water. Leave for 20 minutes until frothy.

❖ Melt the fat in a pan with the milk and beat in the egg. Add with the yeast mixture to the flour and salt, and mix in the currants. Mix to a smooth dough and knead well. Cover and leave to rise until double in size, ½ hour in a warm place. Knock back and knead again.

❖ Divide the dough into 12 pieces, shape each into a small oval and place on a greased baking tray. Cover with a damp cloth and leave to rise for 30 minutes in a warm place. Brush with beaten egg and bake for 25–30 minutes. Cool on a wire rack.

Then, Julia! Let me woo thee
Thus, thus come unto me;
And when I shall meet
Thy silvery feet,
My soul I'll pour unto thee.

ROBERT HERRICK

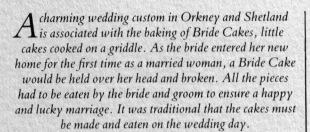

A charming wedding custom in Orkney and Shetland is associated with the baking of Bride Cakes, little cakes cooked on a griddle. As the bride entered her new home for the first time as a married woman, a Bride Cake would be held over her head and broken. All the pieces had to be eaten by the bride and groom to ensure a happy and lucky marriage. It was traditional that the cakes must be made and eaten on the wedding day.

ORKNEY BRIDE CAKES

5 oz/150 g self-raising flour
2 oz/50 g butter, softened
1 oz/25 g caster sugar
1 oz/25 g caraway seeds
3–4 tablespoons milk, to mix

❖ Sift the flour and rub in the butter. Stir in the caster sugar and caraway seeds, and mix to a firm dough with a little milk. Roll out about ½ inch/ 1 cm thick, and cut out a circle using a 7 inch/18 cm plate. Divide into 8 segments.
❖ Cook on a griddle or heavy frying pan over a medium heat for 8–10 minutes, turning once, until golden brown on both sides. Cool on a wire rack.

*I*n Tudor times, it was customary for a bridegroom, attended by the bachelors of the village, to enter church carrying green boughs decorated with bride's lace. It is not certain what type of lace was used, but it is known that the lace was made from a thread known as Coventry Blue. This thread was, in fact, quite coarse, and was manufactured, not surprisingly, in Coventry. The banning of all showy dress by the Puritans stopped this custom and, thereby, brought ruin on the threadmakers of Coventry.
Coventry Blue lace was also used on baptismal gowns and was probably sold throughout the country by itinerant pedlars.

Roses are red
Violets are blue
Carnations are sweet
And so are you.
And so are they
That send you this
And when we meet
We'll have a kiss.

CHILDREN'S RHYME

Make a clove orange in February – one hung in your bedroom will perfume your sleep delightfully and will keep moths away from cupboards and wardrobes. Hang the orange from a doorknob or hook on the wall. It will last for many years, becoming smaller and smaller as it dries out and releases its fragrance. To make a clove orange, take a ripe seville or other thin-skinned orange. Push in cloves, starting at the stalk end (I make the holes initially with a skewer) and working in circles until the whole orange is covered. Mix a teaspoon of orris powder (available from old-fashioned chemists) with a teaspoon of cinnamon and roll the orange in it. Store the orange in a dark place for two weeks, wrapped in white tissue paper. Remove it from the tissue paper and decorate with velvet ribbons, bows or anything else that takes your fancy. To hang up, use a half yard of narrow ribbon or lace, attached by a staple to the top of the orange.

MONDAY BEFORE LENT

Collop Monday

THE MONDAY BEFORE THE START OF LENT, on Ash Wednesday, is known in some areas as Collop Monday. 'Luxury' foods such as meat, eggs and butter were forbidden during Lent, and Collop Monday was the last opportunity for eating meat. Any fresh meat still available would be sliced into steaks and salted to preserve it until the end of the period of fasting – collops, a Scandinavian word, means a slice of meat. People would traditionally eat collops and eggs on this day.

BEEF COLLOPS

1 lb/450 g fillet steak
1½ oz/40 g butter
½ teaspoon finely grated onion
1 teaspoon flour
1 clove garlic, crushed
¼ pint/150 ml good brown stock
1 fl oz/25 ml claret (optional)
Salt and black pepper

❖ Cut the meat into very fine slices. Heat the butter in a frying pan, then fry the grated onion and crushed garlic slowly in the hot butter, stir in the flour and cook for 1 minute. Add the meat, stock and claret if using and simmer gently for 15 minutes. Season. Serve very hot, surrounded by triangles of fried bread.

TUESDAY BEFORE LENT

Shrove Tuesday

PANCAKE DAY

SHROVE TUESDAY is the last day before Lent, which begins on Ash Wednesday. It was customary to make confession and be absolved by the priest on this day 'to shrive' means to absolve in Old English. It is the last day of Shrovetide, which is a carnival period, the last chance for merrymaking before the rigours of Lent. Because it is the day before the fast, Shrove Tuesday is also often known as Fastern's or Fassern's Eve in parts of the North of England and Scotland.

Shrove Tuesday is traditionally a day for fun, feasting and pranks. For centuries cockfighting, football games, truancy and general rowdiness were common, and many communal games still occur on this day. Street ball games such as the St. Columb game in Cornwall or the Royal Shrovetide Football in Ashbourne, Derbyshire attract hundreds of contestants. These games consist of free-for-alls amongst local men, who are loosely divided into two teams. The goals are set at either end of the village and it is a good excuse, during the game and after, for the consumption of a great deal of alcohol and a chance to let off steam! A less violent, but equally popular, custom is the mass skipping that takes place every Shrove Tuesday in Scarborough, where for five hours thousands of people skip along a mile of the Foreshore Road.

Nowadays, Shrove Tuesday is predominantly a day for making pancakes. This was originally intended to use up eggs and butter in the house before Lent began, but fasting for Lent is rarely practised now. Many traditions involving the making – and tossing – of pancakes are still held all over Britain. Pancake races, often in fancy dress, are very popular.

Pancake Tuesday is a very happy day,
If we don't have a holiday we'll all run away,
Where shall we run, up High Lane,
And here comes the teacher with a great big cane.

CHILDREN'S RHYME

*I*n many churches a bell used to be rung on Shrove Tuesday. Originally rung to call the faithful to confession, it became known as the Pancake Bell – letting housewives know it was time to begin preparing the batter. The bell usually rang at eleven or twelve o'clock, so that the batter would be ready for lunchtime. This bell also released people from work and children from school, so that everyone could join in the afternoon's festivities.

PANCAKES

Making a good pancake is an art and a little extra care can produce superb results. The choice of pan is half the battle – I always use a heavy cast iron skillet, which heats well and never sticks.

4 oz/100 g plain flour
Pinch of salt
1 medium egg
½ pint/300 ml milk, or half milk and half water

❖ Sift the flour and salt into a bowl. Beat to a smooth batter with the egg and half the milk or milk and water. Stir in the remaining milk and leave to stand. A few drops of vanilla essence may be added for extra flavour if liked. Leave to stand for 20–30 minutes.
❖ Put the pan on with a tiny knob of clarified butter and test for readiness by holding the palm of your hand over the pan. When you feel the heat rising, the pan is ready.
❖ When the pan and butter are hot, pour in just enough batter to thinly coat the base of the pan. Tilt the pan around quickly to produce an even covering. Fry until golden brown then toss or turn the pancake. Cook again until the second side is golden. Your pancake should look like a lace doily. Sprinkle with caster sugar and lemon juice and serve immediately, or stack on a warm plate, with a layer of greaseproof paper between each pancake, and keep warm over a pan of boiling water.

*I*n Scotland it was usual to eat pancakes with a slice or two of beef on Shrove Tuesday. Make your pancakes as above (omitting the sugar and lemon juice, of course) and put a thin slice of roast beef on top of each. Spread each slice with good tomato sauce, roll up and place in an oven dish. Cover with foil and reheat in a moderate oven. Serve with a garnish of parsley.

A kiss for a woman
A cake for a man
Run to the church
With a frying pan.

CHILDREN'S RHYME

*L*ent Crocking was once a Shrove Tuesday custom. Also known as Shroving or Tiptoeing, children used to (and still do in parts of Britain) visit houses asking in rhyme for pancakes. This was probably first practised by poor villagers who had a right to beg for pancakes on this day. Often they would threaten, if no pancakes were forthcoming, to throw broken crockery at the door. Lent Crocking may also have developed from the custom of law-abiding citizens of the village breaking down the doors of their less reputable neighbours on this day and dragging them through the streets as a penance before Lent.

Here I come, I never came before,
If you don't give me a pancake
I'll break down your door!

LENT CROCKING CHANT

*L*acemakers would work together during the dark, winter days, to economise on the cost of candles. The most experienced lacemakers would have a position of privilege closest to the light, whereas the younger girls, with better eyesight and less skill, would be positioned at the back. The use of candles was strictly regulated, as the cost would have to come from the girls' hard-earned wages. On Shrove Tuesday (whether it fell early or late) their candles were always blown out, not to be lit again until 3rd September, Nutting Day.

Be Shrovetide High or Low
Out the candle we will blow

LACEMAKERS' RHYME

FIRST DAY OF LENT

Ash Wednesday

LENT BEGINS ON ASH WEDNESDAY, a period of forty days' abstinence (excluding Sundays) commemorating Christ's forty days in the wilderness. The word Lent comes from the Anglo-Saxon 'lengentide', which means spring or lengthening of the days. Originally only one meal a day was eaten during Lent, and no meat, eggs or dairy produce consumed at all; nowadays we usually just try to give up one thing – perhaps chocolate, alcohol or smoking. Weddings are still considered unlucky during Lent, as sex was prohibited in this period.

Ash Wednesday is so-named because, in medieval times, bishops used to sprinkle ashes over sack-clothed penitents' heads. Later, priests just made the sign of the cross on the forehead of each member of their congregation, using ashes from the palms from the previous year's Palm Sunday.

In some parts of the country, such as Hampshire and Sussex, children keep a black-budded twig of ash with them all day – if they do not, they are liable to have their feet trampled on by those who do.

The Friday after Ash Wednesday is commonly known as Kissing Friday. On Kissing Day in Yorkshire boys have the right to kiss any girl without rebuke. In the same area, the day after Ash Wednesday is called Fritter Thursday – perhaps because of the simple fried dough fritters that were common fare during meatless Lent.

ASH WEDNESDAY FISH PIE

4 fillets of white fish
½ pint/300 ml milk
Few green peppercorns
Bay leaf
Pinch of salt
Knob of butter
1 oz/25 g butter
1 oz/25 g flour
8 oz/225 g each parsnips and potatoes

OVEN: 180°C/350°F/GAS 4

❖ Put the well washed fish into an ovenproof dish. Cover with the milk, peppercorns and bay leaf, and season with a pinch of salt. Dot with the butter. Cover with foil and bake for 15–20 minutes.

❖ Remove the fish from its liquid and break up with a fork. Put into a buttered, ovenproof dish. Strain the fish/milk liquid. Make a roux with the 1 oz/25 g butter and flour and gradually blend in the milk liquid. Cook, stirring, until the mixture thickens. Lower the heat and simmer gently for 3 minutes. Pour over the fish.

❖ Peel and dice the parsnips and potatoes and cook in boiling salted water for 20–25 minutes until tender. Drain well, mash and sieve. Add a little cream and butter if liked and adjust the seasoning. Pipe over the top of the fish and sauce and return to the oven, 200°C/400°F/Gas 6, for 20–25 minutes until the potato and parsnip mixture browns.

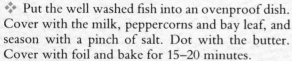

March

St. David's Day

ST. DAVID (or Dewi in Welsh) is the patron saint of Wales, and the 1st March is the Welsh national day. St. David was a 2nd-century monk who founded the Abbey at St. David's, Pembrokeshire, following very strict and austere rules. He became an extremely popular saint, and his shrine was a major centre for pilgrimage in the 12th century.

The Welsh national emblems of the leek and daffodil are obscure in origin, but there are a number of popular theories. There is a story that David led the Welsh to victory against their Saxon foes wearing a leek so that he stood out in battle (in another legend however it is King Cadwallawn). The daffodil is thought to have been chosen because it is like Dafydd, the Welsh name for David. Whatever the reasons, patriotic Welshmen traditionally wear a daffodil or leek on this day.

Leek and Ham Soup

1 medium onion, finely chopped
1 oz/25 g butter
1 oz/25 g flour
1 pint/600 ml white stock or water
6 leeks, cleaned and sliced
4 slices of ham, cut thickly from the bone, chopped
¼ pint/150 ml milk
Salt and black pepper
Single cream

❖ Fry the onion gently in the butter until golden. Stir in the flour and cook for a further minute. Slowly add the stock or water, stirring constantly. Boil until the soup thickens, about 5 minutes. Add the sliced leeks and chopped ham and simmer for 40 minutes. Strain or liquidise with the milk. Return the soup to the pan, add the milk and reheat. Just before serving adjust the seasoning and stir in a little cream.

Bara Brith (Speckled bread)

3 oz/75 g currants
3 oz/75 g sultanas
3 oz/75 g Welsh butter, softened
1 oz/25 g crystallised peel (see page 13)
2 eggs, beaten
¼ teaspoon ground mixed spice
3 oz/75 g brown sugar
12 oz/350 g self-raising flour, sifted
A little warmed honey, to glaze

OVEN: 150°C/300°F/GAS 2

❖ Cover the dried fruit with water in a saucepan and simmer for 15 minutes. Drain well, put in a bowl, and mix in the butter and crystallised peel. Beat in the eggs, spice and sugar. Stir in the flour and mix well.

❖ Bake in a well-greased 2 lb/1 kg loaf tin for 1 hour. Allow to cool for 10–15 minutes in the tin before turning out on to a wire rack and glazing with a little warm honey.

St. Patrick's Day

St. PATRICK IS of course the patron saint of Ireland, and this day is an Irish national holiday. St. Patrick was the son of a Roman tax collector who lived in what is now South-east Wales. At the age of sixteen he was captured by raiders and sold into Irish slavery. Six years later he escaped to Gaul and entered the priesthood – determined to return to Ireland to convert his captors to Christianity. Within ten years he had established churches all over Ireland. He died there in 461 A.D.

The emblem of Ireland is the shamrock; accordingt to legend St. Patrick used a clover to convert the pagan King Loigaire to Christianity, by showing how the three separate leaves united by one stem resembled the Trinity.

Whuppity stourie (or Scoorie) isn't a Welsh tradition, but takes place every 1st March in Lanark, Strathclyde. The kirk (church) bells start ringing at six o'clock in the evening, having been silent since October. As soon as the bells start ringing, locals run around the church three times following the direction of the sun. Originally run by young men whirling (and hitting each other with) their caps, the race is now run by primary school children with paper balls.
In eastern England, the weather on St. David's Day used to be taken as an omen for the type of weather to come – if it is a good day, then the rest of the month will be bad; if it is cloudy or rainy, then March will be sunny. The fact that it is usually cold and windy on St. David's Day is shown in this traditional rhyme – St. Chad and St. Winnold were popular saints in Norfolk and South-west England, and had their respective feast days on 2nd and 3rd March.

First comes David
Then comes Chad
Then comes Winnold, roaring like mad

ST. DAVID'S DAY RHYME
EAST ANGLIA

IRISH SODA BREAD (BROWN CAKE)

A quick and easy bread, which is just right on cold days with a bowl of fragrant, home-made soup.

1½ lb/750 g plain flour
2 teaspoons baking powder
1 teaspoon salt
½ pint/300 ml natural yogurt
¼ pint/150 ml water
1 egg, beaten

OVEN: 190°C/375°F/GAS 5

❖ Mix together the dry ingredients in a bowl. Beat together the yogurt, water and egg in a separate bowl, then mix into the flour to form a stiff dough. Knead well. Form the dough into a soft round cushion and place on a lightly greased baking tray. Cut a cross on the top of the dough and bake for 40 minutes. Take from the oven and wrap in a clean cloth until quite cold.

They say there's bread and work for all,
And the sun shines always there:
But I'll not forget old Ireland,
Were it fifty times as fair.

HELEN SELINA BLACKWOOD
(LADY DUFFERIN)
THE LAMENT OF THE IRISH EMIGRANT

IRISH HAZELNUT HONEY BISCUITS

'Nip the cake' – it was the custom in Ireland to break off a small corner of a freshly baked cake or biscuit as a precaution, to avert bad luck.

3 oz/75 g shelled hazelnuts
5 oz/150 g plain flour
Salt
4 oz/100 g butter, softened
2 oz/50 g caster sugar
4 tablespoons thick honey

OVEN: 190°C/375°F/GAS 5

❖ Toast the hazelnuts in the oven for 10 minutes. Rub off their skins and grind to a powder.
❖ Sift the flour and salt into a bowl. Cream the butter and sugar together and add the ground nuts and flour. Knead lightly. Chill the dough for 30 minutes.
❖ Roll out the dough on a floured surface and cut into 2 inch/5 cm rounds. Put rice paper on to a greased baking tray, place on the biscuits and bake, again at 190°C/375°F/Gas 5, for 7–10 minutes. Cool on a wire rack and then sandwich together with thick honey.

For the great Gaels of Ireland
Are the men that God made mad,
For all their wars are merry,
And all their songs are sad.

G. K. CHESTERTON
BALLAD OF THE WHITE HORSE

In Tudor times it was fashionable to dye lace bright yellow. The dye needed for this fashion was obtained from a lichen gathered from the rocky coast of Ireland and this was mixed with a type of starch. The Irish, first to adopt this fashion, apparently caused quite a sensation when they appeared at the court of Elizabeth I in high starched ruffs of this amazing yellow!

4TH SUNDAY IN LENT
Mothering Sunday

MOTHERING SUNDAY is a long-established celebration but has become especially popular in recent years. In medieval times it was the day on which people visited their 'mother' church, the cathedral of their diocese. Only in the mid-17th century did it become a day for acknowledging human mothers – perhaps it also became confused with Lady Day on the 25th March, which celebrates the Mother of God. Special children's services are still held in many churches around the country on this day.

On Mothering Sunday it used to be the practice to visit one's own mother and give her gifts of flowers and cakes. People working in service away from home were given the day off by their employers – it was quite common in those days for live-in servants not to see their parents for months at a time. Traditionally, Simnel cakes were taken home and bunches of wild flowers such as violets and primroses.

Simnel cakes were originally baked in two layers, with a filling of almond paste in between. The recipe given here can be used for Mothering Sunday or for Easter Day tea. If the cake is to be served at Easter, Victorian tradition holds that the cake should be decorated with eleven marzipan balls to represent the apostles – Judas not being included. It can also be topped with twelve balls to represent the months of the year.

I'll to Thee a simnel bring
'Gainst Thou go a-mothering.
So that when she blesses Thee,
Half that blessing you'll give me.

ROBERT HERRICK

SIMNEL CAKE

The top of this cake may be decorated with a few crystallised flowers or little chocolate eggs, and a few fresh, spring flowers would look especially charming.

1½ lb/675 g sultanas
6 oz/175 g currants
1 pint/600 ml ruby port
Grated rind of 2 large lemons
8 oz/225 g unsalted butter, softened
8 oz/225 g soft brown sugar
4 large eggs
6 oz/175 g crystallised peel (see page 13)
14 oz/400 g plain unbleached flour
1 teaspoon salt
1 teaspoon baking powder
1 teaspoon ground allspice
FOR THE ALMOND PASTE
8 oz/225 g ground almonds
8 oz/225 g icing sugar, sifted
8 oz/225 g caster sugar
1 large egg, beaten
Juice of 1 lemon
TO GLAZE
3 oz/75 g caster sugar
4 tablespoons milk

OVEN: 180°C/350°F/GAS 4

❖ Soak the sultanas and currants overnight in the port. Drain and reserve the port.

❖ Beat together the butter, lemon rind and sugar until light and fluffy. Stir in the eggs, one at a time, beat well and add the chopped, drained peel and dried fruit. Sift the flour into a bowl with the salt, baking powder and mixed spice. Fold into the creamed mixture. If necessary, add 1–2 tablespoons of the reserved port to give a soft dropping consistency.

❖ Grease and line a 9 inch/23 cm round, deep cake tin. Spoon in half the mixture and level the top.

❖ To make the almond paste, mix the ground almonds with the icing and caster sugars. Add the beaten egg and enough lemon juice to give a pliable, but not sticky paste. Cover a working surface with a little sifted icing sugar, turn out paste and knead lightly until smooth. Roll out and cut out a circle the size of the tin.

❖ Place the almond paste on the cake mixture, spoon in remaining mixture and level. Bake in the centre of the oven for 2½–3 hours, turning down the temperature to 150°C/300°F/Gas 2 after 2 hours. Cook until a skewer inserted into the centre comes out clean (allowing for the layer of paste).

❖ Leave the cake in its tin for 15 minutes or so to cool before turning out, to prevent the cake from splitting at the marzipan layer. When the cake is cool, boil together the sugar and milk for the glaze until thick and syrupy, and brush over the top of the cake.

LARGE FAMILY MEALS were usual on Mothering Sunday, with veal, pork, or lamb traditionally being served and with fig puddings, cheesecakes and frumenty to follow. Rather exotic fare for mid-Lent, but this day was also known as Refreshment Sunday, when a lapse was allowed in the Lent fast to commemorate the Feeding of the Five Thousand.

In the counties of Lincoln and Warwick, a chine of pork was traditional for Mothering Sunday lunch.

CHINE OR LOIN OF PORK

3 lb/1.5 kg chine or loin of pork
Few sprigs of parsley
1 egg yolk
6 oz/175 g fresh breadcrumbs
1 oz/25 g melted lard or dripping

OVEN: 220°C/425°F/GAS 7

❖ Boil the chine or loin for 30 minutes in a saucepan of water. Drain and make cuts into the lean part of the meat, about 1 inch/2.5 cm apart. Stuff the sprigs of parsley, stalk first, into the incisions. Brush the chine with egg yolk and coat with the breadcrumbs, patting them on firmly with the palm of your hand. Baste carefully with the melted lard or dripping and roast in the oven for 20 minutes. Reduce the heat to 180°C/350°F/Gas 4 and cook for 20 minutes per pound/450 g, plus 20 minutes over.

MOTHERING SUNDAY FIG PIE

Figs are a common ingredient in Mothering Sunday recipes, perhaps because they symbolise fruitfulness in bearing children!

8 oz/225 g dried figs, soaked overnight in cold water
3 oz/75 g butter, softened
3 oz/75 g soft brown sugar
3 oz/75 g plain flour
2 oz/50 g fresh white breadcrumbs
1 oz/25 g ground almonds
Pinch of cinnamon
1 teaspoon baking powder
1 egg, beaten
3 tablespoons brandy

❖ Drain the figs and mince finely. Cream the butter in a bowl, beat in the sugar, then mix in the figs, flour, breadcrumbs, almonds, cinnamon and baking powder. Stir in the beaten egg and the brandy. Turn into a greased pudding basin. Cover with greaseproof paper and a cloth. Tie with string and steam steadily for 3 hours. Add more hot water to the pan when necessary. Turn out and serve with custard or double cream.

5TH SUNDAY IN LENT
Carling Sunday
PASSION SUNDAY

Passion sunday is the official name for the day on which churches begin their meditations upon the sufferings of Christ. This day is also known as Carling Sunday, a derivation of 'care', which means mourning in Middle English. Altars and crucifixes are draped with purple to announce the beginning of Passiontide.

It used to be the custom all over Britain to eat dried peas on this day, which is why it is often known as Pea Sunday. Grey ('Carling') peas are still prepared and eaten in the North of England and Scotland, where there used to be a number of interesting pea-related customs. In some areas roasted peas were carried up a local hill, together with a drink of well water. At the top of the hill the peas would be eaten and the water drunk. In other areas the peas and water would be taken back down the hill to be made into pea soup. There are many regional versions of the traditional Carling dish of peas, but it is most common, especially in Northumberland, to serve the soaked peas fried in butter and seasoned with salt and pepper.

Pea dishes, an important source of protein in a meatless diet, were often eaten throughout Lent. Because peas were one of the 'approved' foods during Lent, many old people came to believe that they should only eat them at this time, and that if they ate peas before Lent they would be breaking the rules of the Church and choke on their meal.

Why this day in particular became associated with peas is uncertain – perhaps confusion between this festival and an older one called Peasen Sunday.

CARLINGS

8 oz/225 g dried green peas
2 oz/50 g fresh breadcrumbs
1 onion, finely chopped
½ teaspoon mixed herbs
Salt and pepper
1 oz/25 g butter

❖ Soak the peas overnight in cold water. The next day, drain and put into a large saucepan, add 1½ pints/750 ml water and bring to the boil. Boil steadily for 2 hours until the peas are tender. Leave to cool. Mix with the breadcrumbs, onion, herbs and seasoning to make a stiff mixture. Shape into cakes and fry in the butter until brown.

6TH SUNDAY IN LENT

Palm Sunday

PALM SUNDAY celebrates Christ's entry on a donkey into Jerusalem, when people strew his path with palm branches to honour him. Crosses made of palm are still blessed and distributed in many churches today, and carried around the church during the service. This custom has been practised in England since at least the 5th century, and although it was banned during the Reformation as idolatrous, has never died out entirely.

These crosses of palm are nowadays made from imported palm leaves, but before this was possible almost any spring greenery was used. Most common were willow boughs with catkins (known as 'English palm' in some areas). The ancient custom of 'a-palming', which even continued through the Reformation, involved the collection of catkin boughs before dawn on Palm Sunday to decorate villagers' homes.

Crosses of 'palm' were often kept throughout the year for good luck, and in Cornwall were even sold as safeguards against disease. Sometimes the crosses were taken to the local well, and thrown upon the water. If the cross floated the thrower would outlive the year – if not, then he or she could expect to die before next Palm Sunday! Another 'well' custom on this day in the Midlands and northern England involves the drinking of 'holy water' from the wells, mixed with sugar or liquorice. For this reason Palm Sunday is sometimes referred to as Sugar-Cup Day or Spanish Day in these areas (liquorice being seen as Spanish).

A lovely tradition is carried out each year on Palm Sunday in four villages in South Herefordshire, called the Pax Cakes Ceremony. Little flat round cakes are made specially, with a picture of the Lamb of God and the words 'peace and good neighbourhood' on each one. These are given to each member of the congregation after the service. They used to be given with a free mug of ale, but this was stopped in more prudish Victorian times.

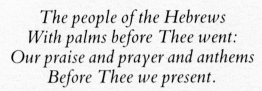

*The people of the Hebrews
With palms before Thee went:
Our praise and prayer and anthems
Before Thee we present.*

HYMNS: ANCIENT AND MODERN NO. 98
ALL GLORY, LAUD AND HONOUR

POND PUDDING

On Palm Sunday it was usual to cook and serve a Pond Pudding. A lovely, and sharper-tasting, variation is the Sussex Pond Pudding – just insert a washed, whole lemon (first pricked all over) in the centre of the pudding and omit the currants. Don't eat the cooked lemon though – it will be bitter.

*4 oz/100 g self-raising flour
2 oz/50 g grated suet
2–3 fl oz/50–75 ml milk
4 oz/100 g butter, softened
2 oz/50 g demerara sugar
2 oz/50 g currants*

❖ Sift the flour into a bowl and stir in the suet. Pour in the milk and mix thoroughly to form a dough. Roll out two thirds of the dough into a large round and use to line a well-buttered 1 pint/600 ml pudding basin.

❖ Beat the butter and the demerara sugar together with the currants and spoon the mixture into the suet crust. Roll out the remaining pastry to make a round lid, place on the bowl and seal well.

❖ Cover the bowl with a double thickness of pleated greaseproof paper and steam steadily in a covered pan for 2½ hours. Top up with boiling water if necessary. Turn out on to a warm dish and serve with custard.

Good Friday

THIS, THE DAY OF CHRIST'S CRUCIFIXION, is the most solemn and holy day in the Christian calendar. No church bells are rung – unless they are tolled in mourning – and altars are stripped of all cloths and adornment. No decorations are hung up in church on this day, except perhaps a branch of mourning yew.

Before the Reformation, some churches ceremoniously took down their crucifix on this day and buried it in a special sepulchre, to be opened again on Easter Day. In other areas a real cross was sometimes carried through the village or town to a hill or public place. Nowadays, Good Friday is for most people a day on which they eat Hot Cross Buns.

In the Christian church's manner of adapting pagan rites to their own ends, these buns are descendants of small cakes made at this time of year in celebration of the spring and the Anglo-Saxon goddess Eostre. Both the Greeks and the Romans had festive spring cakes too, which bore a similarity to our own Hot Cross Buns. Their cross was a symbol of the sun – a circle bisected by two right-angle lines, cutting the bun into four quarters, representing the four seasons. At one time all bread was marked with a cross to help the dough rise, but this was frowned on by the church after the Reformation except for special holy cakes.

Hot Cross Buns were thought, in olden times, to have holy powers. A bun would be hung from the ceiling of the house to protect all within from harm. If a member of the household (or one of the animals, for that matter) became ill, a small amount would be grated into warm milk or water. This was thought to cure most ailments. If the bun went mouldy, then disaster was sure to strike the house during the coming year.

The recipe given here is adapted from the spiced buns baked and sold during Tudor times. As late as 1784, bakers could only sell spiced buns such as these on special occasions – weddings, christenings and burials and on holy days such as Good Friday and at Christmas. If a baker ignored this decree he would be punished and all his bread would be taken and given to the local poor.

HOT CROSS BUNS

These are so good, compared with the commercial varieties, that it really is worth the effort involved to make them. This recipe will make 12 buns.

1 oz/25 g fresh or 1 tablespoon dried yeast
2 oz/50 g soft brown sugar
¼ pint/150 ml lukewarm milk
4 tablespoons lukewarm water
1 lb/450 g plain flour, sifted
1 teaspoon salt
1 teaspoon ground mixed spice
½ teaspoon ground cinnamon
4 oz/100 g currants
2 oz/50 g crystallised peel (see page 13)
2 oz/50 g butter, softened
1 egg, beaten
2 oz/50 g granulated sugar
3 tablespoons milk

OVEN: 220°C/425°F/GAS 7

❖ Cream the yeast, mixed with 1 teaspoon of the sugar, until liquid, then blend in the milk and water and add 2 tablespoons of the sifted flour. Mix well and leave in a warm place until frothy (20 minutes).
❖ Sift the remaining flour, salt and spices into another bowl. Add the soft brown sugar, currants and peel. Add to the yeast mixture and beat in the butter and beaten egg. Mix to a soft but not sticky dough that leaves the bowl clean. Cover with a cloth and leave to rise until doubled in size.
❖ Turn the dough on to a floured board, knead lightly and then divide into 12 equal portions. Shape each into a round bun and stand on a greased and floured tray. Cover and leave to rise for 30 minutes or until the dough feels springy.
❖ Cut a deep cross into the top of each bun with a sharp knife and bake in the centre of the oven for 20–25 minutes. Transfer to a wire rack. Dissolve the granulated sugar in the 3 tablespoons of milk and boil for 2 minutes. Brush the warm buns twice with this syrup to glaze.

A hot cross bun has been hung up in a public house called the Widow's Son in the London Docklands every Good Friday since the early 19th century. The pile, added to every year, probably totals nearly two hundred by now – some of which have been transferred to the cellar, in various states of decay! This Widow's Bun Collection commemorates a poor widow who originally lived on the site now occupied by the pub. Every Good Friday she baked a Hot Cross Bun in expectation of the return of her sailor son – who, alas, never came home. When the public house was subsequently built, part of the terms of the lease was that a sailor should hang a bun each year in memory of the widow's devotion.

Little work used to be done on Good Friday as it was such an unpropitious day, although it was once considered a good day for planting and sowing since the Devil was thought to have no power over the soil. Certainly no smith would ever hammer in a nail today, and in some parts of the country housewives would do no washing as it was believed that the water or clothes on the line would suddenly be found tainted with blood.

Once a day of general fasting and abstinence, fish is still traditionally eaten on Good Friday. Fish Days used to be very common in the Middle Ages, and until the 16th century every Friday and Saturday used to be fish-only days. If no fresh fish was available, salted had to be used. Nowadays, fortunately, there is an abundant supply of many varieties of fish, and this recipe for baked salmon is both traditional and delicious.

GOOD FRIDAY BAKED SALMON

Serve this pie hot with boiled potatoes and broccoli.

4 thick salmon steaks
1 lb/450 g puff pastry
½ Spanish onion, chopped
3 oz/75 g butter
2 oz/50 g mushrooms, chopped
2 oz/50 g fresh brown breadcrumbs
Pinch of ground allspice
1 egg, beaten
4 tablespoons milk
Salt and white pepper
2 tablespoons dry sherry
3 tablespoons lemon juice
1 egg, beaten, to glaze

OVEN: 200°C/400°F/GAS 6

❖ Skin the salmon steaks. Roll out two thirds of the pastry on a floured board and line a shallow baking tin; put the pastry case in the refrigerator to cool. Fry the onion gently in 2 oz/50 g of the butter until soft and golden. Add the mushrooms and breadcrumbs and fry for a further 2–3 minutes, stirring all the time. Remove from the heat and add the spice, egg and milk, stirring well. Season to taste and put aside to cool.

❖ Arrange the salmon steaks in the pastry case and coat with the mushroom mixture. Bring the sherry, remaining 1 oz/25 g butter, and lemon juice to the boil in a pan, cool slightly and pour over the filling. Roll out the remaining pastry to make a lid, place over the filling and brush with the beaten egg to glaze. Bake for 45 minutes.

EASTER SUNDAY
Easter

EASTER DAY FALLS between 21st March and 25th April, the date depending on the first full moon of spring. It is calculated as the first Sunday after the full moon on or after the 21st March, but if the full moon falls on a Sunday, then Easter is the following Sunday.

Easter celebrates Christ's resurrection, and the defeat of sin, darkness and death; churches are decked with flowers or evergreens, and bells are rung triumphantly.

The name Easter is sometimes linked with pagan cults of the Saxon spring goddess Eostre, especially since the eggs popular at Easter are ancient symbols of spring, rebirth and renewal of life. The Pascal lamb slaughtered at the Jewish Passover has been incorporated into the Christian symbol of Christ as a sacrificial lamb, and of course the traditional lunch at Easter is roast lamb.

This spring lamb recipe is perfect for an Easter family lunch, perhaps served with mint sauce, potatoes and dwarf beans. It includes rosemary for remembrance – the herb that represents the Virgin Mary. The blue of the rosemary flowers is said to be the colour of the Virgin's robes.

Loveliest of trees, the cherry now
Is hung with bloom along the bough,
And stands about the woodland ride
Wearing white for Eastertide.

A. E. HOUSMAN
LOVELIEST OF TREES

ROAST LAMB WITH ROSEMARY AND GARLIC

Use leg or shoulder of lamb,
about 12 oz/350 g meat on the bone per person
2–3 cloves of garlic, sliced
3–4 sprigs of fresh rosemary
1 oz/25 g butter, melted

OVEN: 230°C/450°F/GAS 8

❖ Wipe over the joint of lamb with a damp cloth. Cut slits in the skin and rub with salt and pepper. Insert alternate sprigs of rosemary and slivers of garlic into the slits. Dribble melted butter over the joint and stand in a roasting tin.

❖ Put the lamb in the centre of the preheated oven and reduce the heat immediately to 180°C/350°F/ Gas 4. Roast for 25 minutes per pound/450 g plus 25 minutes over for a joint cooked in the English manner; 15–20 minutes for pinker meat. Do not baste.

EGGS HAVE BEEN PART OF EASTER celebrations for a long time. In the Middle Ages they were even claimed as an Easter tithe by the parish priest, and villagers brought eggs to him to be blessed. The blessing of special eggs still occurs in many parishes. There are lots of Easter egg customs practised today all over the country, in particular the giving of decorated eggs to family and friends, and perhaps (if you have children) hiding them in the garden for a treasure hunt or egg-rolling down hills.

It is easy and great fun to make your own decorative coloured eggs on Easter day. Use white eggs and boil them in various vegetable waters to obtain different colours and effects. Onion skins wrapped and tied around the eggs will give an orange marbled effect, or you can boil eggs in beetroot water for a pink colour, or spinach water for green. For an especially pretty and delicate effect, wrap each egg in flower petals and then cover them with onion skins; tie carefully in place and boil. Remove the onion skins and dry gently. Rub lightly with olive oil and polish with a soft cloth. Pile your decorated eggs on to a flat china dish or fine basket for serving.

'Pace-egging' or 'Jollyboying' is a popular tradition for many children, who dress up and soot their faces and go knocking on people's doors asking them for Easter eggs in rhyme. They are often given little coloured eggs in return. In Anglesey, the children clap two pieces of slate together to make a clacking noise and chant: 'Clap, clap, ask for an egg, small boys on the parish' – a pretence at being begging paupers, presumably.

Now we're jolly pace-eggers all in one round,
We've come a pace-egging, we hope you'll prove kind.
We hope you'll prove kind with some eggs and some beer,
For we'll come no more near you 'til it's next year.

PACE-EGGING RHYME

SOMERSET EASTER CAKES

These are sometimes known more specifically as Sedgemoor Easter Cakes – the story goes that the Duke of Monmouth was fleeing from the Battle of Sedgemoor and fell into a ditch. A local woman, thinking he was a poor peasant down on his luck, baked him these biscuits to strengthen him. This recipe will make 24 cakes.

8 oz/225 g plain flour
4 oz/100 g butter, cut into pieces
4 oz/100 g caster sugar
4 oz/100 g currants
1 teaspoon ground cinnamon
1 egg, beaten
2 tablespoons brandy
Milk, to mix

OVEN: 180°C/350°F/GAS 4

❖ Sift the flour into a bowl and rub in the butter until the mixture resembles breadcrumbs. Stir in the sugar, currants and cinnamon, then mix in the egg and brandy and enough milk to give a soft dough that falls reluctantly from the spoon. Spoon the mixture into well greased bun tins and bake for 20–25 minutes.

In your Easter Bonnet
With all the frills upon it
You'll be the sweetest lady
In the Easter Parade.

POPULAR SONG

*I*n parts of north-west England and the Welsh Border counties, a strange custom called 'Lifting' or 'Heaving' used to take place on Easter Monday. Strong young men were chosen to be the 'lifters', and visited each house in the village. They would make a chair with their arms and the females of each house would sit in this in turns. They were then hoisted up three times and turned around. On Easter Tuesday, the custom would be reversed and the women would lift the men in retaliation. The origins of this practice are thought to have been some mystical fertility rite, but it later came to symbolise the resurrection. In Herefordshire, the lifters would sing 'Jesus Christ is risen again' as they entered each house. In some places a chair decorated with ribbons and greenery would be used. Lifting had to cease at noon and many shy young ladies would lock themselves indoors until twelve, in the hope that they would escape the indignity of being 'lifted'. Seen as rude and unseemly in Victorian times, the custom fell into decline.

April

April Fool's Day

APRIL FOOL'S OR ALL FOOLS' DAY, beloved by children everywhere, is a day for unlicensed jokes, pranks, hoaxes and horseplay. The origins of this day are unknown, but the customs and rhymes are similar all over Britain. In Scotland it is called Huntingowk Day, which is a derivation of 'hunting the gowk' (cuckoo).

There are many, many jokes practised on April Fool's Day, such as sending friends on fool's errands to buy pigeon milk, elbow grease, or a left-handed screwdriver. Pennies are stuck to floors, or banknotes tied with 'invisible' thread so that when people try to pick them up they are whisked out of reach . . . There are oft-repeated cries of 'Your shoelace is undone' or 'There's something stuck to your back'. Stink bombs are set off, books balanced on doors so that they fall on unsuspecting teachers, and notes are left around reading: 'A duck in a pond, a fish in a pool, whoever reads this, is a big April Fool.' When you fall for a joke, you are roundly teased as an 'April Fool', or with 'Ever been had, April Fool?'.

In Scotland the unlucky child is sent on a fruitless journey from person to person, carrying a sealed message which reads, to the recipient, 'Don't you laugh and don't you smile; hunt the gowk another mile'. The victim is then sent on to yet another destination . . .

April Fool jokes, however, must stop at the stroke of noon or the prankster becomes the fool.

Huntingowk's past
And you're the ass.
Up a tree and down a tree
You're a fool as well as me.

CHILDREN'S RHYME
SCOTLAND

APRIL FOOL AFTERNOON, in parts of the Midlands, is 'Tripping-up Time' – which speaks for itself. The following day, 2nd April, is for some persistent Scottish jokers 'Taily Day', where notes are pinned to the unfortunate's back saying 'kick me hard' and other pleasantries.

There are no traditional foods associated with April Fool's Day, but it would be rather nice to serve a fruit fool as a dessert at teatime.

RHUBARB FOOL

1 lb/450 g young rhubarb
Juice of 1 lemon
3–4 tablespoons caster sugar
¼ pint/150 ml double cream, whipped

❖ Clean, trim and slice the rhubarb. Put into an enamelled pan with the juice and sugar. Cover and bring to simmering point, then cook for 8–10 minutes depending on the thickness of the rhubarb. Leave to cool, then purée through a sieve or in a processor (if it is young it should not have any strings). Mix the rhubarb with the cream and chill before serving.

Set for friends your nonsense snares
Catch them and be caught by theirs.

ELEANOR FARJEON

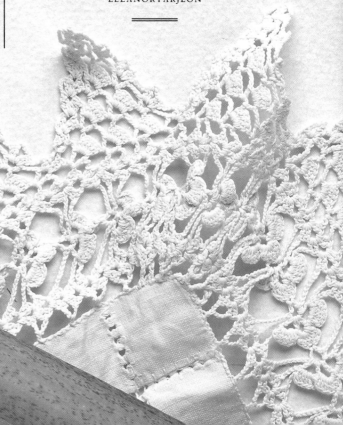

APRIL 23

St. George's Day

ST. GEORGE is of course the patron saint of England (as well as, you may be surprised to hear, Venice, Genoa, Portugal, Catalonia and Greece), and today is the English national day. St. George in fact only became patron saint in the 13th century, superceding Edward the Confessor. He is an obscure figure (some people even doubt whether he really existed at all), but there are generally accepted stories about his life.

St. George is thought to have been a Roman Christian from Cappadocia in Asia Minor, who lived in the late 3rd century. On his travels through Libya he came across a town which was being terrified by a fierce dragon. In order to stop the dragon eating their sheep, the townspeople sacrificed young maidens to it, drawn by lot. As St. George arrived, the king's daughter Cleodolinda had been chosen, and had been dressed as a bride and tied at the mouth of the dragon's sea cave. St. George charged and defeated the dragon, and the princess led it back meekly to the city by her girdle. The king and his subjects were so amazed by St. George's feat that they converted to Christianity.

St. George was first made patron of the Order of the Garter in 1348 and was then declared patron saint of England. After the victory (attributed to him) at Agincourt, the festival of St. George became a day for great civic celebration, and in the olden days jousting was held, with knights challenging all comers to feats of skill. The day ended with feasting, and, presumably, much drinking of ale and mead.

Today, civic processions and pageants are still held on 23rd April, and mumming plays on the theme of St. George and the Dragon are performed in many parts of the country. To celebrate this English day – which is also Shakespeare's birthday – here are two traditional English country recipes.

Spring cowslips were once gathered by village maidens and made into cowslip balls, for carrying or as decoration for the home. This is a lovely idea to copy, and you could buy a packet of wild cowslip seeds and plant them in the garden. Any you are lucky enough to find growing wild should be left in peace, as cowslips, along with many other of our disappearing wild flowers, are now a protected species.

St. George he was for England,
And, before he killed the dragon,
He drank a pint of English ale
Out of an English flagon.

G. K. CHESTERTON

OLD ENGLISH SAUSAGES

These traditional sausages are very spicy and far superior to bought varieties.

4 oz/100 g lean pork, minced
4 oz/100 g lean veal, minced
4 oz/100 g beef suet, grated
2 oz/50 g fresh white breadcrumbs
Grated rind of ½ lemon
½ nutmeg, grated
1 teaspoon chopped parsley
1 teaspoon mixed herbs
Salt and black pepper
2 eggs, beaten
1 oz/25 g butter
1 tablespoon oil

❖ Combine the meats and suet in a bowl and stir in the breadcrumbs, lemon rind, nutmeg and herbs. Season and bind with the eggs. Mix well.
❖ Form the mixture into sausage shapes, using a little flour to help you.
❖ Melt the butter and oil in a frying pan and fry the sausages for about 10 minutes, turning a few times. Drain on a paper towel and serve hot.

EVESHAM APPLE PIE

1 quantity of shortcrust pastry, made with
8 oz/225 g flour (see recipe on page 22),
sweetened with 2 teaspoons caster sugar and
¼ teaspoon ground cinnamon
2 lb/1 kg Bramley cooking apples
2 tablespoons orange marmalade
½ teaspoon ground cinnamon
A knob of butter (optional)
2–4 oz/50–100 g brown sugar

HEAT THE OVEN TO 200°C/400°F/GAS 6

❖ Roll out two thirds of the shortcrust pastry and line a flan ring set on a baking tray. Set aside to rest in the refrigerator.
❖ Peel, core and slice the apples and stew in a little water until a thick pulp is obtained. Remove from the heat and stir in the marmalade and cinnamon. Add a knob of butter if a rich texture is preferred, taste and add brown sugar if necessary. Leave to cool.
❖ Fill the pastry case with the apple mixture. Roll out the remaining pastry to make a lid, put on the pie and bake in the oven until golden. Sprinkle with caster sugar and return to the oven until the sugar melts and forms a glaze. Serve with whipped cream, or a wedge of English cheese. ('Apple pie without cheese is like a kiss without a squeeze', as the saying goes.)

APRIL 25

St. Mark's Day

Sᴛ. ᴍᴀʀᴋ was one of the four Evangelists. He wrote the second gospel and is supposed to have founded the city of Venice. His day was once the occasion for a number of superstitious beliefs and customs. Like Hallowe'en and Midsummer's Eve, St. Mark's Eve was considered to be a night when the frontier between the realms of the living and the dead dissolved, and it used to be thought that if you dared to stand in the churchyard for three hours over midnight you would see the future ghosts of those in the parish who were to die in the year to come, walking in a procession through the church porch. However, you had to be careful not to fall asleep, or you were doomed to a similar fate.

There were variations on this belief in different parts of the country – in some places it was thought you had to visit the churchyard three years in succession before you would see the spirits. In East Anglia it was thought that only those ghosts who didn't re-emerge from the church would die, and in other areas the opposite was believed.

Other – less sombre – superstitions relate to St. Mark's Day. Girls who wanted to see an image of their future sweetheart would sometimes bake a Dumb Cake the evening before. In complete silence, they would mix an eggshell-full of salt, an eggshell-full of flour and an eggshell-full of barley meal to a dough with a little water. They had to be alone and bake it before the fire just before midnight, when their sweethearts would come and turn the cake.

*H*oniton lace at its best consists of sprigs of flowers and leaves gracefully worked and attached to a lace net ground. It produces a beautiful and distinctive fabric. Queen Victoria's wedding lace was made by the lacemakers of Beer, in Devon, and the dress cost £1,000. It was made of Honiton sprigs connected by open-work net. The butterfly here is made from Honiton lace.

*A*pril is the month in which people have always eagerly awaited the arrival of the cuckoo, indicating that spring is truly on its way. Because April is also a month of uncertain weather, the coming of the cuckoo was linked in folklore to the weather. A late spring was crucial to the fortunes of the farmer, since it meant that little spring grass was available for livestock, and there was a risk of late frosts that could ruin a crop.

When the cuckoo sings in an empty bough
Keep your hay and sell your cow.

OLD FARMERS' SAYING

RHUBARB WINE

Before 'scientific' wine-making equipment became available, country wines were made in this simple but effective way.

15 lb/7 kg rhubarb
1 gallon/4.5 litres boiling water
2½ lb/1.25 kg sugar
1 teaspoon fresh yeast

❖ Clean, trim and slice the rhubarb. Put in a deep bowl and pour the boiling water over it, and mash well with a potato masher. Leave to soak until the next day. Strain off the liquid and press the rhubarb to extract all the juice. Stir in the sugar and yeast and leave to ferment before racking and bottling.

May

May Day

MAY 1ST, MAY DAY OR GARLAND DAY, is the time set aside for celebrating the spring and rejoicing in the signs of renewal all round. For the ancient Celts, it marked the beginning of summer, when they took their livestock up to the hills to graze again after being kept in the valleys over the winter. Long before the time of Red Square parades and the singing of the 'Nationale', the people of England gathered on their village greens for May Day revels and to dance around the Maypole.

The Maypole is a symbol of virility – the dance probably began as a rite in honour of the Sun God, god of fertility. The pole was traditionally sixty to eighty feet high, and painted with brightly coloured rings or spirals – it would stand on the green all year round, waiting to be redecorated with ribbons and greenery. The shorter Maypole we often see today, with bright ribbons, which become plaited in the course of the dance around it, is in fact a 19th-century import from southern Europe, as is the idea of a child May Queen. The prettiest maidens of the village would dance around the Maypole, and the loveliest was chosen as May Queen, often accompanied by a King, and crowned with hawthorn blossoms. The May Queen is thought originally to have represented Flora, the Roman goddess of spring.

Hawthorn, or 'May' blossoms once bedecked every door and window on May Day, and milk-maids would drape the horns of their cows with garlands of the sweet, white flowers. In North-western and Midland counties, 'May birchers' would circulate the parishes on May Eve, distributing various kinds of branch to all the houses – hawthorn in blossom was always a compliment, but other kinds of thorn were indicators of scorn.

❖Another popular tradition among young maidens on May Day was to rise with the dawn and wash your face with the dew, to ensure a fair complexion – and that you would marry the first man you met afterwards.

❖IHere are two recipes on an alcolohic theme, closely associated with May Day. The first is a wine cup, thought to have originated in Germany – it is traditionally offered to travellers and visitors on May Day.

MAY CUP

1 bottle sweet white wine
2 bottles sweet cider
1 wine glass brandy
Fresh orange slices
1 bunch Ladies' Bedstraw

❖ Mix all together, cover well and chill for 2 hours or more. Strain and serve in tall glasses.

MAY LIQUEUR

May blossoms
2 tablespoons granulated sugar
1 bottle brandy

❖ Gather the May blossoms in full sunlight, and trim off their tiny stalks – you should use only the flower heads. Pack them into a wide-mouthed jar, sprinkle over the sugar and pour on the brandy. Seal tightly and put on a window-sill in full sunlight until warm. Shake well to dissolve the sugar and then leave in a dark cupboard for 3 months. Strain very gently into clean bottles, seal and leave for at least 4–6 months before sampling.

When daisies pied and violets blue
And lady-smocks all silver-white
And cuckoo-buds of yellow hue
Do paint the meadows with delight.

WILLIAM SHAKESPEARE
LOVE'S LABOUR'S LOST

MAIDS OF HONOUR

In remembrance of the maidens dancing around the Maypole since time immemorial, you could bake these sweet tartlets for tea on May Day. They are thought to have been served originally at the court of Henry VIII to Anne Boleyn and her own maids of honour, although some say they were invented for Queen Elizabeth I at Richmond Palace. This will make about 15 tarts.

8 oz/225 g shortcrust pastry (see page 22)
2 tablespoons raspberry jam
2 oz/50 g butter, softened
4 oz/100 g caster sugar
1 egg, beaten
A few drops almond essence
4–5 oz/100–150 g ground rice

OVEN: 200°C/400°F/GAS 6

❖ Roll out the pastry and cut into circles with a pastry cutter. Line tart tins with the pastry circles and smear a little raspberry jam into each. Partly cook the tarts in a hot oven for about 10 minutes, then take out and leave to cool. Reduce the oven temperature to 180°C/350°F/Gas 4.
❖ Mix together the butter, sugar, egg and almond essence, and add enough ground rice to make a stiff paste. Put a spoonful of mixture in each tart case and return to the oven for 25–30 minutes until well risen and golden.

Sweet, masking May, in white or red
Her snowy cloud of blossoms spread.

WALTER CRANE
FLORA'S FEAST

*I*t used to be customary for young men to wear fine new linen shirts on May Day, on to which their girlfriends would have sewn ribbons and bows. The men would then form a team, headed by the Garland Bearer, to dance on May Day. Just before May Day the Garland Bearer would borrow items of value from local farmers – silver spoons, watches, etc. These would be attached to the garland – a long pole with a triangular frame attached. The frame would be covered with strong white linen and the spoons would be sewn on in various patterns. The top of the pole would be crowned with a large silver object, such as a cup or tankard. When the garland was completed it would be left at the home of the farmer who had contributed the most silverware and from there it would be collected early on May Day morning. This garland, together with its team of dancers, would then tour the parish, collecting alms as it went.

All around the Maypole we will trot
From the very bottom to the very top
On the first of May.
First come the buttercups
Then come the daisies
Then come the gentles
Then come the ladies.

OLD MAY DAY SONG

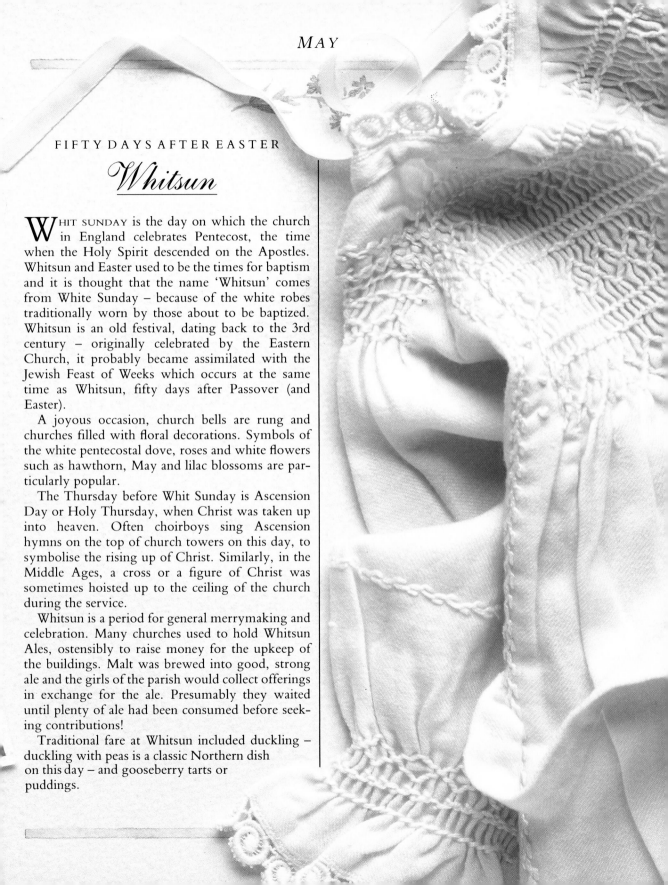

FIFTY DAYS AFTER EASTER

Whitsun

WHIT SUNDAY is the day on which the church in England celebrates Pentecost, the time when the Holy Spirit descended on the Apostles. Whitsun and Easter used to be the times for baptism and it is thought that the name 'Whitsun' comes from White Sunday – because of the white robes traditionally worn by those about to be baptized. Whitsun is an old festival, dating back to the 3rd century – originally celebrated by the Eastern Church, it probably became assimilated with the Jewish Feast of Weeks which occurs at the same time as Whitsun, fifty days after Passover (and Easter).

A joyous occasion, church bells are rung and churches filled with floral decorations. Symbols of the white pentecostal dove, roses and white flowers such as hawthorn, May and lilac blossoms are particularly popular.

The Thursday before Whit Sunday is Ascension Day or Holy Thursday, when Christ was taken up into heaven. Often choirboys sing Ascension hymns on the top of church towers on this day, to symbolise the rising up of Christ. Similarly, in the Middle Ages, a cross or a figure of Christ was sometimes hoisted up to the ceiling of the church during the service.

Whitsun is a period for general merrymaking and celebration. Many churches used to hold Whitsun Ales, ostensibly to raise money for the upkeep of the buildings. Malt was brewed into good, strong ale and the girls of the parish would collect offerings in exchange for the ale. Presumably they waited until plenty of ale had been consumed before seeking contributions!

Traditional fare at Whitsun included duckling – duckling with peas is a classic Northern dish on this day – and gooseberry tarts or puddings.

DUCKLING WITH PEAS

2 ducklings
2 oz/50 g seasoned flour
2 oz/50 g butter
2 pints/1.2 litres brown stock
Salt and pepper
1 lb/450 g fresh shelled peas
2 lettuces, finely chopped
1 bunch mixed thyme, parsley and sage
¼ nutmeg, grated
¼ pint/150 ml double cream
2 egg yolks

OVEN: 180°C/350°F/GAS 4

❖ Truss the ducklings and dust with the seasoned flour. Heat the butter in a pan and brown the birds all over to seal. Put into a roasting tin on a rack and roast in the oven for 30 minutes.

❖ Pour off the fat and put the birds in a large saucepan. Add the stock, salt and pepper, and simmer for 15–20 minutes. Add the peas, lettuce and herbs. Cover and simmer for a further 40 minutes or until the ducklings are tender.

❖ Remove the bunch of herbs, lift out the ducklings and keep them warm in a low oven. Press the cooking liquid and vegetables through a sieve, or blend in a liquidiser. Put the purée in a pan, add the nutmeg to taste and blend in the cream and egg yolks. Heat gently, but do not boil. Adjust the seasoning, pour over the ducklings and serve, garnished with a little parsley.

GOOSEBERRY PUDDING

8 oz/225 g self-raising flour
½ teaspoon salt
1 teaspoon baking powder
4 oz/100 g freshly grated beef suet
¼ pint/150 ml cold water
1½ lb/675 g gooseberries
4 oz/100 g brown sugar

❖ To make the suet crust, sift the flour, salt and baking powder into a bowl. Add the finely grated suet and mix well. Add enough of the water to make a firm paste, and knead until smooth.

❖ Roll out two thirds of the suet pastry and use to line a well-greased 2 pint/1.5 litre pudding basin. Half fill the basin with half the gooseberries, sprinkle on half the quantity of sugar and then add the rest of the fruit. Sprinkle on the remaining sugar. Roll out the remaining pastry into a round to form a lid. Place on the basin, and seal well with a little water.

❖ Cover with a double thickness of greaseproof paper, pleated to allow for expansion, and steam for 3–3½ hours, topping up with hot water if the level drops too much. When turned out the suet pudding should be dry, golden and crisp on the outside.

When Yew is out
Then Beech comes in
And many flowers beside,
Both of a fresh and fragrant kin
To honour Whitsunside.

ROBERT HERRICK
CEREMONIES FOR CANDLEMAS EVE

*M*any old folkloric customs used to be practised at Whitsuntide, and it is still a popular time for spring fêtes and fairs. Some events have now been transferred to the Whitsun Bank Holiday which falls at the end of May, but a number still take place at Whitsun itself.

A very attractive tradition that occurs in some areas of Britain, but in particular in Derbyshire, is that of well dressing. There used to be many holy wells and springs in Britain with reputedly magical or curative powers, some of which are still kept up and attract pilgrims. These wells were often originally consecrated to pagan deities but many were rededicated to Christian saints and, frequently, the Virgin Mary. The water from these wells and springs used to be thought to be particularly effective at special times such as Easter or Whitsun and especially Ascension Day. At these times, usually Whitsuntide, many of the wells are garlanded with flowers and bedecked with ribbons. Some, such as the village wells at Tissington in Derbyshire, are decorated with incredibly complicated mosaics of biblical scenes, using only natural materials. At Wirksworth, also near Derby, there are as many as nine wells, each decorated with a different design.

MAY 29

Oak Apple Day

O AK APPLE OR ROYAL OAK DAY was once a time for great national celebration and festivity. It is the day on which Charles II was restored to the throne, and it became popularly known as Oak Apple Day due to the story of his escape from the Roundheads. Fleeing from pursuers after the Battle of Worcester, Charles hid in an oak tree near Boscobel House at Wolverhampton. Although this actually happened on 4th September, it naturally became linked with the day of his restoration, decreed as a day of national thanksgiving by Parliament in 1660.

Because the Puritans had forbidden 'pagan' pleasures and festivities such as May Day, many newly-revived May Day customs became linked with the celebrations on Oak Apple Day. In Devon, garlanded dolls called 'May Babies' were once carried by girls around village streets, and young boys would carry sticks dressed with flowers to welcome summer. Other traditions such as collecting hawthorn blossom at dawn and morris dancing also occurred on Oak Apple Day.

A sprig of oak is the Royalist badge, and until quite recently everyone was expected to wear the token on this day. Oak leaves and apples were fastened to lapels (and even gilded leaves were once fashionable in some Dorset villages). Churches, homes and even railway trains in Victorian times were decorated with oak. Children still sometimes challenge each other to reveal their token, and if they are found not to be wearing one, a number of penalties have to be paid – usually pinching or being stung by nettles. For this reason Oak Apple Day is known as Pinch-Bum Day to many children. Popular legend has it that Charles II had to be pinched by his companions when hiding in the tree in order to keep awake, which henceforth justified similar action by schoolchildren all over the country! In some parts of England, where oak apples were

known as shick-shacks, this day was also known as Shick-Shack Day and those not wearing an oak sprig were called 'jick-jacks'.

Beer and plum pudding are traditionally on the menu on Oak Apple Day for the pensioners at the Charles II Royal Hospital in Chelsea, which seems an appropriate English dish for such a day.

Twenty-ninth of May,
Royal Oak Day;
If you don't give us a holiday
We'll all run away.

CHILDREN'S RHYME
NORTH ENGLAND

PLUM DUFF

This Plum Pudding was also known as 'Baby's Bum' because of the mark left by the string in the pudding. A good dish for Pinch Bum Day . . .

4 oz/100 g fresh breadcrumbs
4 oz/100 g plain flour, sifted
4 oz/100 g grated suet
4 oz/100 g brown sugar
Generous teaspoon baking powder
4 oz/100 g mixed dried fruit
1 teaspoon ground mixed spice
Milk, to mix

❖ It is better to buy suet from the butchers for this recipe – remove the membranes and grate coarsely. Toss in 2 oz/50 g of the sifted flour.

❖ Put all the ingredients into a bowl and mix well with a wooden spoon. Add enough milk to make a stiff dough.

❖ Sprinkle a clean pudding cloth or tea towel with flour, and shape the dough into a thick roll. Place on the cloth, leaving a pleat of material at either end. Roll up and tie with string at each end and loosely around the centre. Put the pudding into a pan of boiling water and boil for 1½ hours, adding more boiling water when necessary.

❖ Cut the string, remove the cloth and turn on to a warm dish. Pour over a little warmed golden syrup and serve with cream.

June

Barnaby bright
Barnaby bright
Longest day
Shortest night

TRADITIONAL

St. Barnabas' Day

St. BARNABAS' (or Barnaby's) Day used to be an important date in the church calendar, although it is largely forgotten nowadays. Only a few major saints' days were celebrated during June (the others being St. John's Day on the 24th and St. Peter's on the 29th), partly because this was a month too busy with hay-making and sheep-shearing for time to spare on festivals.

Before the calendar change of 1752, 11th June was the longest day of the year. This is now the 21st June, but a few old Midsummer rites were once linked to St. Barnabas' Day. Garlands of flowers – roses, lavender, rosemary and a sweet woodruff – were worn and used to decorate the church and the home. Because June is the time for hay-making, St. Barnabas is often depicted with a hay-rake.

JUNKET FOR OLD MIDSUMMER'S EVE

❖ Warm 1 pint/600 ml milk to blood temperature (98°F/32°C) and pour into a serving dish. Stir in a dessertspoon of rennet and a tablespoon of sugar. Leave the junket in a fairly warm place until set, then chill slightly before serving.

JUNE 23

Midsummer's Eve

ALTHOUGH THE SUMMER SOLSTICE, technically the day when the sun climbs highest in the sky and shines for the longest hours, occurs on 21st June, Midsummer celebrations have traditionally commenced on the evening of 23rd June.

On the night before Midsummer's Day, until at least the 18th century, bonfires to celebrate the solstice used to be lit on hilltops up and down the land soon after sunset. A common custom was for people, after the flames had died down, to leap over the bonfires in the hope of changing their luck. This act perhaps stems from ancient purification rites, given the cleansing properties of fire.

Midsummer has always been regarded as a powerful time for fortune-telling, divination, fairies and magic. As the embers of bonfires died down, some people would look into the fire and foretell the future.

MIDSUMMER SYLLABUB

Syllabub was originally a refreshing, foaming drink prepared by milking a cow directly into a bucket of fruit wine, cider or ale. In later times, it was discovered that a mixture based on cider, lemon and whipped cream produced a richer, more sophisticated syllabub. Perhaps you could serve it with gooseberries, said in Somerset to ripen at Midsummer.

¼ pint/150 ml dry cider
Rind and juice of 1 lemon
1 oz/25 g caster sugar
½ teaspoon grated nutmeg
¼ pint/150 ml whipping cream
¼ pint/150 ml double cream

❖ Combine the cider and lemon rind in a large bowl. Stir in the sugar and nutmeg.
❖ Pour in the whipping cream and the double cream, whisk until thick and then add the lemon juice. Spoon into wine glasses and chill before serving.

Why, this is very midsummer madness.

WILLIAM SHAKESPEARE
A MIDSUMMER NIGHT'S DREAM

On Midsummer's Eve take a black velvet pincushion. In one side stick your name with the smallest pins you can find. On the other side with large pins make a cross surrounded with a circle. When you go to bed, put the pincushion in your right-foot stocking and hang it at the foot of the bed. Having accomplished this task, all your future life is supposed to pass before you in a dream.

JUNE 24

Midsummer's Day

MIDSUMMER'S DAY, which in the ancient calendar was celebrated on 4th July, was for centuries one of the main festivals in the country. It marked the half-way point of the year and celebrated the abundance and mystery of Nature.

This has always been a time for gathering special flowers and herbs with magic properties from the fields and hedgerows. These plants were believed to ward off the attentions of mischievous spirits, and were woven into garlands and worn on the head or around the neck, and even placed around the necks of favourite farm animals. It was especially important to pick the pungent yellow herb St. John's Wort (known by some as 'chase-devil') on Midsummer's Day, as it was believed to repel evil as well as being an effective cure for many ailments. In Wales, it was customary to place a sprig of St. John's Wort above the door of the house on Midsummer's Day as a protective measure. Rowan was also powerful against witches, and was burned for safety in parts of Cumbria on this day.

Regarded as an auspicious time for divination, many fortune-telling customs have been recorded. Some people used to believe that if a piece of Orpine (also known as 'Midsummer's Men') picked on Midsummer's Eve wilted overnight, disappointment was certain and possibly even death for the one who picked it.

Many of the customs traditionally associated with Midsummer have now died away, although it is still a very popular date for fairs and summer fêtes. A festive summer pudding seems appropriate for this day, and an old-fashioned recipe is given opposite.

Then doth the joyful feast of St. John the
Baptist take his turn,
When bonfires great with lofty flame in
every town do burn;
And young men rounds with maids do
dance in every street,
With garlands wrought of motherwort, or
else with vervain sweet.

THOMAS KIRCHMEYER
16TH CENTURY

QUEEN MAB'S SUMMER PUDDING

Try not to overdo the blackcurrants, as their strong
flavour will mask that of the other more delicate
fruits.

6–8 slices stale white bread, with the crusts cut off
1½ lb/675 g soft fruits – blackcurrants,
strawberries, raspberries, etc.
2 tablespoons water
5 oz/150 g sugar

Line a 1½ pint/1 litre pudding bowl with the
slices of bread. Cut more if necessary to completely
cover the bottom and sides.

❖ Wash and prepare the fruit and put into a saucepan with the water and sugar. Gently boil until the
sugar melts and the juices begin to run but do not
allow the fruit to disintegrate.

❖ Spoon the fruit into the prepared dish and make
a lid with the remaining bread. Put a saucer or small
plate that fits inside the dish on top and weigh down
with a heavy tin or jar. Chill for 8 hours or more.

❖ Remove the weights and plate and turn out the
pudding on to a china plate or dish. Serve with
whipped cream.

JUNE 29
St. Peter's Day

ST. PETER is often considered to be the most important apostle; called 'The Rock' he is seen by Roman Catholics as the father of all Christians. Popularly believed to have lived and preached in Rome, he was crucified there and his body is now reputedly buried in St. Peter's Basilica. The 29th June is his feast day, although many of the festivals held on this day do not seem to bear much relation to the Saint at all.

Haystrewing ceremonies used to be held in many parts of the south-eastern Midlands on St. Peter's Day, and still are in some churches although the custom has been gradually declining – especially when compared to the similar, elaborate rush strewing processions held in other parts of the country during the summer (see page 92 for more details). Originally designed to provide a simple, cheap floor covering that was also pleasant and scented, the strewing of hay and rush over the church floor became a ceremonial event. The strewings took place at various times of the year in different parts of the country.

Sometimes hayfields were donated by worthy parishioners for the sole purpose of providing hay for church strewing, bequests which still survive in some areas today. There is a story that the Petertide strewing at the church in Old Weston, Huntingdonshire, was due to the bequest of a certain local man who became so irritated by the clumping of labourers' boots in church that he ensured a permanent supply of hay to soften the sound!

Villagers in Appleton, Cheshire, still practise an interesting ceremony called Bawming the Thorn. This used always to be performed on St. Peter's Day, but it can now occur at any time in late June. A special hawthorn bush stands in the centre of Appleton village, protected by a fence. On the appointed day this bush is decorated with ribbons and flowers by local children, who then dance around it singing Bawming songs. 'Bawming' comes from an old word meaning 'anoint', and so this 'sacred' bush is being blessed symbolically.

Of all the trees that grow so fair,
Old England to adorn,
Greater are none beneath the Sun,
Than Oak, and Ash, and Thorn.

RUDYARD KIPLING
A TREE SONG

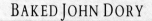

BAKED JOHN DORY

John Dory is also often known as St. Peter's fish, due to the black thumbprints on either side of its head – which are said to be the mark of St. Peter.

4 John Dory fillets
8 oz/225 g shrimps
2 oz/50 g button mushrooms
1 teaspoon anchovy essence
1 egg, beaten (optional)
salt and pepper
1 tablespoon white wine or cider

OVEN: 200°C/400°F/GAS 6

❖ Wash the fish and wipe it dry. Cut into oblong strips. Finely chop the shrimps and mushrooms, combine in a bowl and add the anchovy essence. Moisten, if necessary, with a little beaten egg.

❖ Put a little of this mixture on to each strip of fish and roll up into little parcels. Put into a buttered ovenproof dish, season with salt and pepper and moisten with the white wine or cider.

❖ Cover with buttered greaseproof paper and cook for about 15 minutes, depending on the thickness of the fillets.

July

Thomas à Becket's Day

Thomas à Becket was made a saint in 1173, three years after he had been murdered by Henry II's men in Canterbury Cathedral. Originally a close friend of the King, he became his enemy by vigorously defending the rights of the Church against the Crown after he was made Archbishop of Canterbury. After his death Thomas was represented as the defender of the faith and miracles were supposed to occur at his tomb.

Henry VIII later tore down his shrine and announced that St. Thomas was no longer a saint. However his cult took a while to die out, and his feast day, 7th July, is still remembered in name in parts of the country although no specific celebrations occur.

In Cornwall, Bodmin once celebrated St. Thomas à Becket's Day with a drinking festival followed by Riding Games on the Monday – which had little to do with horses, but were rather Cornish wrestling matches.

In Devonshire, at Lapford, the church is dedicated to St. Thomas à Becket and on the first Sunday after St. Thomas à Becket's Day a Revel would be held, for which every farmhouse would prepare a pestle pie. These pies were usually very large and would be like our modern raised pies, filled with ham, tongue and chicken. On the Monday there would be a fair.

ELDERFLOWER VINEGAR

10–13 sprays of elderflower
1 pint/600 ml white wine vinegar

❖ Pick the flowers when they are in full bloom and snip the flowers from the stalks. Make sure they are insect-free too. Put the flowers into a jar, pack them down well and pour over the vinegar. Close, and leave in a sunny place for 2-3 weeks, then taste to see if the flavour is sufficiently developed. When it is ready, strain and decant the vinegar into bottles and store in a dry cupboard.

*T*atting used to be known as knotting. In Victorian
*times, the term 'frivolity' became widely used
instead – that being considered a more genteel name.*

JULY 15

St. Swithin's Day

S<small>T. SWITHIN WAS BISHOP OF WINCHESTER</small> in the 9th century and became famous for his lack of pomp, his financial administration and for allegedly performing a miracle in the town's marketplace when he made a basket of broken eggs whole again. After his death, his fame spread and grew, and on 15th July, 971 A.D., his bones were moved from the churchyard to a new shrine in the recently completed cathedral in Winchester. It is believed that the Saint protested at the move by 'weeping', causing torrential rain to fall continually for forty days; hence the legend arose:

St. Swithin's Day, if thou dost rain
For forty days it will remain.
St. Swithin's Day, if thou be fair
For forty days, 'twill rain no mair.

TRADITIONAL

There was also a belief concerning the growth and ripening of apples on St. Swithin's Day. It was thought that if it rained on this day, the Saint was christening the apples and there would be a good harvest. In many areas, no-one would eat an apple before St. Swithin's Day, but after that date fallen fruit was picked up and jam made.

EVE'S APPLE JAM

An apple jam recipe for St. Swithin's Day, named after the original apple picker!

To each 1 lb/450 g peeled and cored apples, add:
¼ pint/150 ml water
12 oz/350 g preserving sugar
Finely grated rind of 1 lemon
Juice of ½ lemon

❖ Thinly slice the apples and put into a saucepan with the water. Bring to the boil, reduce the heat and simmer gently for 10–15 minutes until the fruit is soft and pulpy. Add the sugar, lemon rind and juice and heat slowly, stirring until the sugar dissolves. Bring to the boil and boil briskly for 10–15 minutes.

❖ Remove the pan from the heat. Pour the mixture into sterilised, dry jars and cover and store.

Stolen sweets are always sweeter,
Stolen kisses much completer,
Stolen looks are nice in chapels,
Stolen, stolen, be your apples.

JAMES HENRY LEIGH-HUNT
SONG OF FAIRIES ROBBING AN ORCHARD

JULY 20

St. Margaret's Day

S T. MARGARET WAS A POPULAR SAINT in the Middle Ages, although she was later taken off the list of official canonisations. The story is that she was the daughter of a prince, brought up as a shepherdess and converted to Christianity. Refusing the advances of a pagan governor, she was thrown to a dragon who swallowed her. A cross materialised inside the dragon, splitting its belly so that St. Margaret was able to step out unscathed. She is thus seen as the patron saint of safe childbirth!

Her feast day was remembered in many parts of the country, but mostly in Gloucestershire. A pudding was made in this area in honour of St. Margaret – quaintly known as Heg Peg Dump, it was traditionally a dumpling containing wild plums. Heg for hedgerow, Peg for Margaret, and Dump for dumpling!

HEG PEG DUMP

FOR THE SUET CRUST PASTRY
8 oz/225 g self-raising flour
½ teaspoon salt
1 teaspoon baking powder
4 oz/100 g finely grated suet
¼ pint/150 ml cold water

FOR THE FILLING
1 lb/450 g plums or damsons, stoned
8 oz/225 g cooking apples, peeled, cored and sliced
6 oz/175 g granulated sugar
1 tablespoon stale sponge cake crumbs
1 tablespoon water

❖ Sift the flour, salt and baking powder into a bowl. Add the suet and mix together lightly. Add the water and mix to a soft paste. Turn out on to a floured surface and knead until smooth and pliable.

❖ Roll the dough out thinly, saving about a third to make the lid, about ⅛ inch/3 mm thick and use to line a 2 pint/1.2 litre pudding basin.

❖ Fill the pastry-lined basin with alternate layers of the fruit, sugar and cake crumbs. Pour in the water. Moisten the edges of the pudding pastry with water and cover with a lid rolled from the remaining pastry. Press the edges firmly together to seal.

❖ Cover with buttered greaseproof paper or foil and tie securely. Steam steadily for 2½-3 hours, topping up the water level with hot water when necessary. Serve from a basin, with a jug of single cream.

JULY 25

St. James' Day

ST. JAMES WAS A FISHERMAN summoned by Jesus to become one of his disciples. He preached with St. John and was martyred in 43 A.D. By the 9th century, a legend has grown up that he had preached in Spain and that he was buried at Compostela. This became a famous place of pilgrimage and the scallop shell, his symbol, became the badge of pilgrims who visited his shrine.

By the old form of the calendar, before it was changed in 1752, St. James' Day was the start of the official oyster season. This is now really 5th August, but old oyster ceremonies still occur on St. James' Day itself. In the oyster fishing town of Whitstable, an annual service is held on this day on St. Reeves' Beach to bless the oyster fishing boats, their crews and the sea. This old ceremony (it dates back to at least the early 19th century) is similar to many other coastal ceremonies of blessing the seas and fishermen.

In London there was an age-old custom of local lads building small grottoes with oyster shells at the sides of the roads. These 'St. James' Grottoes' were once built solely with oyster shells, but later usually just made with stones and flowers. Pennies were collected from passers-by with the request 'Please sir, remember the grotter'.

There is an old saying that 'He who eats oysters on St. James' Day will not want for money during the year', and so (despite the expense) this may be a good excuse for a dish of oysters today.

He had often eaten oysters,
but had never had enough.

W. S. GILBERT

SCALLOPED OYSTERS

24 oysters
1 oz/25 g butter
1 oz/25 g flour
¼ pint/150 ml white stock
2 tablespoons cream
Salt and pepper
Fresh white breadcrumbs

OVEN: 200°C/400°F/GAS 6

❖ Open the oysters carefully, remove them from their shells and reserve their liquor. Remove the beards from the oysters.

Simmer the oysters for about 10 minutes in oyster liquor, plus a little water if necessary. Put the oysters into a basin and strain the liquor on to them.

❖ Melt the butter in a saucepan, add the flour and cook, stirring, for 2–3 minutes. Add the stock and oyster liquor and stir until the sauce thickens. Add the cream and oysters and season to taste.

❖ Butter 6 scallop shells and fill with the oysters and sauce. Cover with the breadcrumbs. Pour a little melted butter over each and bake for 15–20 minutes until brown and bubbling.

Please remember the grotto,
It's only once a year.
My father's gone to sea,
My mother's gone to fetch him back,
So please remember me.

CHILDREN'S CHANT
LONDON

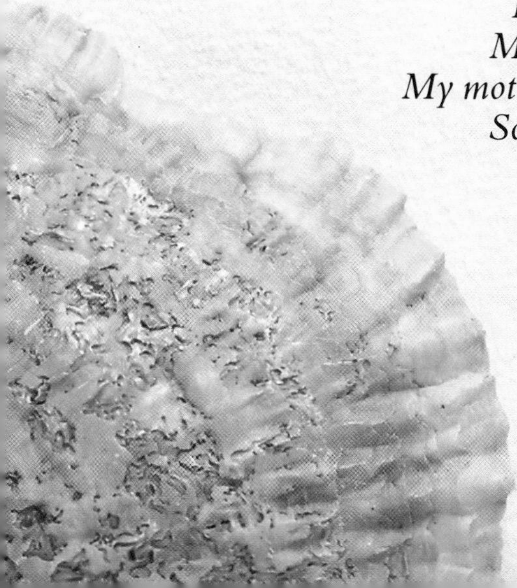

August

Lammas Day

THIS IS AN OLD CHURCH FESTIVAL, with ancient origins, though it is generally forgotten nowadays. Lammas Day, August 1st, was once an important quarter day in the Celtic year, and was called Lughnasad Day after their god Lugh. Harvest festivals relating to Lughnasad were very common in Scotland.

The name Lammas probably comes from a corruption of 'loaf-mass', due to the breads made at this time made with the first cut corn of the harvest and blessed by the priest. Some people also think the name could be derived from 'lamb-mass', as lambs were once dedicated at church on this day.

Lammas Day used to be a time for foretelling marriages and trying out partners. At many Lammas Fairs it was also the custom for two young people to agree to a 'trial marriage' lasting the period of the fair – usually eleven days – to see whether they were really suited for wedlock. At the end of the fair, if they didn't get on, the couple could part – a remarkably modern concept!

Large sheep fairs were traditionally held in many parts of the country on Lammas Day, and these were occasions for general festivity and games. Semi-common grazing lands were also opened for public use, lasting until Candlemas.

LAMPLE PIE

This traditional lamb pie seems a suitable dish for Lammas Day – serve with boiled potatoes and cauliflower.

8 oz/225 g shortcrust pastry
1 oz/25 g dripping
1 lb/450 g lean lamb, cut into small cubes and dried on kitchen paper
½ nutmeg, grated
1 teaspoon rosemary
Salt and black pepper
¼ pint/150 ml brown stock
8 oz/225 g cooking apples, peeled, cored and sliced
Beaten egg, to glaze

OVEN: 200°C/400°F/GAS 6

❖ Roll out two thirds of the shortcrust pastry and use to line a metal pie plate.

❖ Melt the dripping in a frying pan and fry the lamb until brown on all sides. Add the nutmeg, rosemary and seasoning and stir in the stock. Cook for 15–20 minutes. Leave to cool and then drain.

❖ Put into the lined pie dish layers of the apple and the drained meat. Roll out the remaining pastry to make a lid, press on to the pie and decorate with pastry leaves made from the trimmings. Glaze with the beaten egg.

❖ Bake for 25–30 minutes until golden brown. Use any stock left over from cooking the meat to enrich the gravy.

VICTORIAN SUMMER PUDDING

1 pint/600 ml fresh milk
Rind of 1 small lemon
2 oz/50 g toasted almonds
½ oz/15 g powdered gelatine
4 oz/100 g caster sugar
½ pint/300 ml double cream
6 egg yolks
2 oz/50 g glacé cherries, chopped
2 oz/50 g crystallised fruit, chopped finely

❖ Put the milk into a saucepan with a small piece of lemon rind and the toasted almonds. Heat to just below boiling point, remove from the heat and cover. Leave for half an hour .

❖ Remove the lemon rind from the milk, and stir in the gelatine. Add the sugar and double cream. Heat very gently and whisk in the well-beaten egg yolks. Continue to heat gently until the mixture thickens. Pour into a bowl and leave to cool slightly. Stir in the crystallised fruit and glacé cherries. Pour into an oiled jelly mould and put into the refrigerator to set. Turn out on to a pretty dish and serve with Raspberry Sauce.

RASPBERRY SAUCE

6 oz/175 g raspberries
2 oz/50 g icing sugar, sifted

❖ Put the raspberries through a nylon sieve and sweeten to taste with the sifted icing sugar.

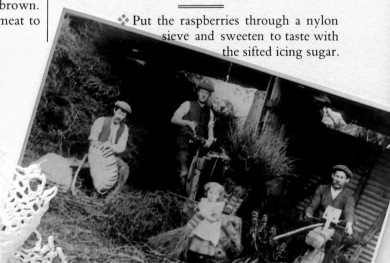

AUGUST 5

St. Oswald's Day

S<small>T. OSWALD IS THE LOCAL PATRON SAINT</small> of Grasmere church in the Lake District, and his feast day is on 5th August. On the Saturday nearest this day a famous rushbearing ceremony takes place. Children and choristers parade through the village to the church carrying traditional 'bearings' – large decorations based on biblical themes made from rushes and flowers. Six young girls, called 'rush maidens', also carry a special hand-woven linen sheet filled with rushes. After the procession and a special service in the church, the participants indulge in pieces of Grasmere gingerbread, each stamped with an image of St. Oswald.

Nearby towns in the Lake District have similar rushbearing ceremonies around this time. These ceremonies date back to the days when most churches had stone or earth floors rather than floor-boards and central heating. Fresh hay, straw and rushes used to be spread over the church floor to make it softer underfoot (and knee), slightly warmer and sweeter to the smell. This covering was renewed before major festivals, and particular-ly before the church's dedication day, which usually fell during the summer months when the rushes and hay were plentiful and in their prime. Eventually these strewing ceremonies became festivals in their own right and still take place in some parishes, par-ticularly in the north-western counties. These rush-bearing processions always involve the local children and are picturesque affairs.

SPECIAL GINGERBREAD

The Grasmere gingerbread is made to a secret recipe and so cannot be given here, but this version is equally delicious.

1½ lb/675 g plain flour
½ oz/15 g bicarbonate of soda
1 oz/25 g ground ginger
½ oz/15 g ground cinnamon
8 oz/225 g soft brown sugar
1½ oz/40 g dried fruit
8 oz/225 g butter
1 lb/450 g treacle or syrup
¼ pint/150 ml of brandy
1 egg, beaten
A little milk mixed with egg yolk, to glaze

OVEN: 180°C/350°F/GAS 4

❖ Sift the flour with the bicarbonate of soda and spices into a basin. Add the sugar and dried fruit and mix together.

❖ Heat the butter with the syrup in a pan until melted, take off the heat and stir in the brandy. Gradually stir in the dry ingredients, with the beaten egg to give a smooth dough.

❖ Spoon the mixture into a large 9 × 12 inch/23 × 30 cm tin, greased and lined with greaseproof paper, and bake for 80–90 minutes. About 10 min-utes before it has finished baking, brush the top with a little milk mixed with egg yolk. Put it back in the oven to finish baking.

❖ Allow the gingerbread to cool in the tin for 10–15 minutes before turning out on to a wire rack. Cut into squares, then wrap in foil and keep in an airtight tin.

AUGUST 12

The Glorious Twelfth

THE GAME SEASON OFFICIALLY STARTS on August 12th, when top restaurants rush the first grouse down from the moors of Scotland to meet the demands of the discriminating gourmet.

Having been brought up in the suburbs of a city, I had no chance to sample game, and the stories I had heard of game needing to be hung until rotten before it was tender enough to eat reinforced my view that it was a taste I had no desire to acquire. However, having lived for the past seventeen years in the hunting and shooting county of Staffordshire, I have learnt to appreciate game dishes, although I still prefer my game a little short of high!

ROAST GROUSE

1 grouse per person
FOR EACH GROUSE
2 oz/50 g rowanberries
2 oz/50 g butter, melted
2 rashers unsmoked bacon
1 teaspoon fresh or dried rosemary or heather flowers
1 tablespoon whisky
Salt and black pepper

OVEN: 190°C/375°F/GAS 5

❖ Stir the heather or rosemary into the whisky and leave to marinate for an hour or more.
❖ Wipe the birds with a damp cloth and pat dry. Season well inside with salt and black pepper. Mix the rowanberries with melted butter and fill the cavity of the bird.
❖ Pour the whisky and heather or rosemary into a shallow roasting tin and put in the grouse. Bard the breast of each bird with the bacon rashers. Cook for 30 minutes.
❖ Remove the bacon and baste each bird well. Sprinkle with a little flour and cook for a further 10 minutes to brown them.

ROWANBERRY JELLY

8 oz/225 g rowanberries
1 lb/450 g crab apples or cooking apples
1 lb/450 g granulated sugar for each 1 pint/600 ml liquid
1½ pints/750 ml water

❖ Wash the rowanberries well and slice the apples, peel and pips included. Put both into a saucepan with the water. Cover and simmer until the fruit is soft. Strain through a cloth.
❖ Measure the juice and for each pint/600 ml add 1 lb/450 g sugar. Bring to the boil in a large heavy pan until it reaches setting point (220°C). Pour into warm, dry jars and cover. Store in a cool, dry place.

AUGUST 24
St. Bartholomew's Day

St. BARTHOLOMEW, or Bar-Tolmai (son of Tolmai), lived and died in the 1st century in Palestine. He is reputed to have been flayed alive and is, therefore, known as the patron saint of butchers and tanners.

In London, a great fair used to be held at Smithfield, dating back to 1133, in honour of the nearby hospital of St. Bartholomew founded by Henry I's jester. This fair brought together many traders, which provided much-needed income for the hospital, but it also provided an excuse for much raucous behaviour, and the fair was eventually banned in 1855 because it was said that it was an offence against public dignity and morals. At this fair the forerunners of today's toffee apples were served – windfall apples, skewered on sticks and dipped in thick honey. An appropriate tradition, since St. Bartholomew was also the patron saint of bee-keepers and honey-makers.

A number of other customs relating to St. Bartholomew's Day are still practised today. In the Kent port of Sandwich, the founding of the 13th-century hospital and chapel of St. Bartholomew is celebrated on this day. Local children run a race around the chapel's walls and are rewarded with a currant bun, and the adults present receive a 'St. Bart's Biscuit' which is imprinted with the hospital's seal. Another tradition, supposedly relating to St. Bartholomew but more likely to have its origins in an ancient fertility god ritual, is the Bartle Burning that takes place at West Witton in Yorkshire. An effigy named Bartlemas is processed around the village and burnt.

FRUIT CHEESE

This delicious fruit 'cheese' is actually a purée of blackberry and apple that sets firm, and is particularly attractive if set in a mould and turned out. Serve with cream or spread on bread.

2 lb/1 kg apples, washed
2 lb/1 kg blackberries, cleaned
1 lb/450 g sugar for each lb/450 g of pulp

❖ Cut up the apples roughly and put with the blackberries in a pan. Just cover with water and stew, stirring occasionally, until the apples have gone mushy. Sieve and weigh the pulp, and add the appropriate amount of sugar. Put back in the pan and boil, stirring all the time. When it has thickened, cool and pot like jam.

How doth the little busy bee
Improve each shining hour,
And gather honey all the day
From every opening flower!

ISAAC WATTS
AGAINST IDLENESS AND MISCHIEF

TOFFEE APPLES

Allow 2 apples per person. This recipe will make enough toffee for about 12 apples.

12 apples
5 tablespoons water
4 oz/100 g honey
2 teaspoons vinegar
1 lb/450 g granulated sugar
2 oz/50 g butter

❖ Pour the water and honey into a saucepan and gradually bring to the boil.
❖ Add the vinegar, sugar and butter and heat slowly, stirring all the time, until the butter and sugar melt. Bring to the boil and boil gently for 2 minutes. Turn down the heat slightly and continue to boil for 15 minutes or until the sugar thermometer registers 138°C–142°C/280°F–290°F.
❖ Push a stick into each apple and dip it into the toffee mixture. Leave to cool on a buttered tray. Any remaining toffee can be poured into a buttered tray and then broken into pieces when it sets.

BARTLEMAS BEEF

A dish closely associated with St. Bartholomew's Day is Bartlemas Beef.

3 lb/1.5 kg brisket of beef
¼ teaspoon each of ground nutmeg, ginger,
cinnamon, cloves and mace
1 teaspoon salt

OVEN: 180°C/350°F/GAS 4

❖ Rub the beef well with a mixture of the spices and salt. Put into a close-fitting earthenware dish and cover with water. Braise for 30 minutes per pound/450 g until tender.
❖ Serve the beef very hot with parsnips and potatoes, or cold with spiced mustard.

THROUGHOUT AUGUST

August Wakes

WAKES USED TO BE FEAST DAYS held to honour local town saints, centred around the parish churches dedicated to the saint. They took place at many different times of the year, although summer tended to be most popular. Sometimes these feast days were called wakes, sometimes just feasts or, in the West Country, revels.

Wakes gradually became a very important part of the calendar in the Midlands and the north of England, as they began to be synonymous with a town's annual holiday. August has always been the main time for outdoor festivities, sports, fairs and games, and so many wakes weeks occurred at this time.

The term wake refers to the medieval custom of staying awake in the parish church all night before the saint's feast day, in order to hear mass at dawn. In the beginning wakes were quite sombre occasions, and parishioners would fast and do penance. However after the Reformation more emphasis began to be placed on revelry and much merry-making took place on the eve of the saint's day. Because of the increasingly lewd behaviour of many young men on these supposedly holy occasions the celebrations were transferred to the daytime, and usually took the form of a market fair to raise money for the church.

Many places served their own special wake or feast day dish. A popular dish in the north is still known as 'Hindle Wakes', derived from Hen de la Wake (Hen of the Wake).

HINDLE WAKES

5 lb/2 kg boiling chicken
1 large onion, peeled and quartered
1 bouquet garni
1 pint/600 ml white stock
FOR THE STUFFING
4 oz/100 g prunes
6 oz/175 g fresh white breadcrumbs
¼ teaspoon mixed herbs
1 oz/25 g grated suet
1 egg, beaten
FOR THE SAUCE
½ teaspoon powdered gelatine
2 oz/50 g butter
1½ oz/40 g flour
Juice of 1 large lemon
Salt and pepper

❖ Soak the prunes for the stuffing in tea overnight. The next day, drain and then stone the prunes. Mince or chop them and combine with the breadcrumbs, herbs, suet, egg and salt and pepper.

❖ Stuff the chicken with the prune mixture. Sew up the openings and truss the limbs. Put the bird into a large stew pan with the onion, bouquet garni and stock. Bring to the boil and skim if necessary. Cover and simmer for 1½–2 hours.

❖ Lift out the chicken, drain well and leave to cool. Strain the stock and set aside.

❖ Dissolve the gelatine in 2 tablespoons of stock according to the instructions on the packet. Melt the butter in a saucepan and stir in the flour. Cook gently for 1 minute, stirring all the time, but do not allow to brown. Gradually add the stock and bring to the boil, stirring constantly. Blend the lemon juice into the sauce and adjust the seasoning. Allow to cool slightly then stir in the gelatine. Leave to cool, stirring occasionally.

❖ Take out the trussing string from the chicken and remove the skin. When the sauce thickens, gently spoon it over the bird and leave it to set. Decorate with lemon, prunes and watercress.

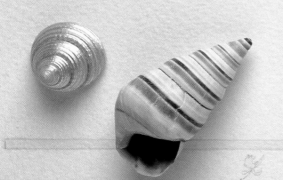

FEASTEN CAKES

At wakes in Cornwall, saffron-coloured cakes
known as Feasten Cakes were served. These are
delicious served with clotted or whipped cream.

1 lb/450 g plain flour
½ teaspoon ground cinnamon
4 oz/100 g unsalted butter, softened
¾ oz/20 g or 2 teaspoons dried yeast
2 oz/50 g sugar
Large pinch of saffron, infused for about 20 minutes
in ¼ pint/150 ml hot milk
6 fl oz/175 ml clotted cream
2 eggs, beaten
4 oz/100 g currants
Milk, to glaze

OVEN: 190°C/375°F/GAS 5

❖ Sift the flour and cinnamon into a bowl. Rub in
the butter.

❖ Cream the yeast with 2 teaspoons of the sugar.
Strain the saffron milk and beat in the cream,
then mix with the yeast. Leave in a warm place for
20 minutes until bubbles form on the surface.

❖ Pour the yeast mixture into the flour with the
beaten eggs. Add the currants and remaining sugar
and knead well. Cover and leave in a cool place for
the dough to rise slowly until double in size. Knead
again briefly then knock back and shape into 8 small
buns or cakes and flatten slightly. Cover with a
damp cloth and leave to prove so that the dough
springs back when pressed, 20–30 minutes.

❖ Arrange on a lightly greased baking sheet.
Brush the tops of the buns lightly with milk and
sprinkle with a little sugar.

❖ Bake for 25 minutes.

❖ Take out and cool on a
wire rack.

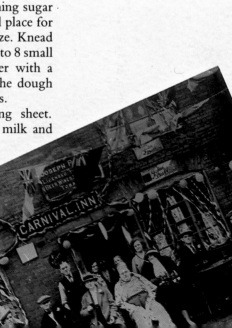

September

Harvest Festival

The timing of the harvest varies according to weather conditions and location, but festivals are held all over the country at the end of summer to celebrate the bringing-in of the crops. Most of these festivals now take the form of a religious service in the local parish church. In times past they were much more of a pagan celebration and took place in the fields and farms as each stage and crop of the harvest was completed successfully.

Apart from being a time for hard work, harvest was also a time full of mysticism and ritual. At the start of the harvest, communities would appoint a strong and respected man of the village as their Lord of the Harvest. He would be responsible for negotiating the harvest wages and terms, organising the fieldworkers and setting the work pace, calling for rests and meal breaks, and the urging on of any slackers. The men would be spread across the field and would move in a line, scything the crop as they went. Behind them followed the women and older men who would gather and bind the cut corn. After it had been stacked and dried, it would be made into ricks or collected on carts and taken back to the barns to be stored.

Great ceremony was always attached to the

gathering of the last sheaf of corn, and a great Harvest Shout was raised by the reapers as it was cut. The last sheaf was treated with special respect and used to make Corn Dollies, as it was believed to harbour the Corn Spirit itself. It was then placed on top of the final load of corn and carried back into the village in triumph. In some places, it would be fashioned into a Corn Lady or Kern Baby, dressed in white robes and garlanded with coloured ribbons. The Corn Dolly would be planted in the first new furrow the following spring on Plough Monday, so that its spirit would be released and ensure another good harvest. During the winter months, the Corn Dolly was believed to protect the family from evil spirits and from need.

At the end of the harvest each farmer would give a huge supper for all who had helped bring in the crop. Having stored the last load of corn, the team of harvesters would follow their elected Lord of the Harvest into supper.

SHROPSHIRE FIDGET PIE

This is a substantial dish and will probably not need any other vegetables. It was often served as a supper dish for the harvesters.

8 oz/225 g shortcrust pastry (see page 22)
4 medium potatoes
3 onions
3 cooking apples
3 rashers of sweetcure gammon
1 tablespoon brown sugar
Salt and pepper
½ pint/300 ml vegetable stock
1 egg, beaten, to glaze pastry

OVEN: 200°C/400°F/GAS 6

❖ Butter a pie dish and line it with the pastry, keeping back enough dough (about a third) to cover the pie later.
❖ Slice the potatoes and onions very thinly. Peel, core and slice the apples. Take the rind from the gammon and cut the rashers into strips. Arrange all these ingredients in layers in the pastry-lined pie dish. Sprinkle on the sugar and season well, then pour in the stock.
❖ Roll out the remaining dough to make a pastry lid, brush with the beaten egg and decorate with the pastry trimmings.
❖ Bake the pie for 30 minutes, then reduce the heat to 160°C/325°F/Gas 3 and bake for a further 30 minutes.

Hip! Hip! Hip! for the harvest home,
Now we've taken the last load home,
I ripped my shirt and I teared my skin,
To get my master's harvest in.

WARWICKSHIRE HARVEST SONG

THE USUAL FARE AT HARVEST SUPPER was boiled beef or mutton with potatoes, followed by a wheat pudding of some description. In some areas, a dish called whipod was served, consisting of rice, white bread, raisins, treacle and currants, which must have been very similar to a bread pudding of today. Special harvest breads were made, often in the shape of an ear of wheat. Great quantities of ale were consumed and the wages, which were often very small, would be handed out. It was probable that the harvesters would be less likely to grumble about their low wages if their stomachs were full and their heads muddled by ale.

Many farmers had their own harvest jugs for use at this time, which usually bore their names and a verse composed by a local wit. The gathering of the harvest was celebrated with music, singing and dancing as well as the hearty supper. Games were played, one of which required six strong men to stand in two rows of three facing each other. They would link arms and a man and a woman would be laid side by side across the linked arms and then tossed in the air. This was thought to be some type of fertility ritual associated with the gathering-in of the harvest.

The potter fashioned me complete
As plainly doth appear
For to supply the harvest men
With good strong English Beer

INSCRIPTION ON NORTH DEVON HARVEST JUG
CITY MUSEUM, PLYMOUTH

DAMSON AND APPLE TANSY

This is an adaptation of a 15th-century recipe, which is perhaps best described as a fruit purée with egg and breadcrumbs.

8 oz/225 g damsons
8 oz/225 g cooking apples
2 oz/50 g butter
2–3 oz/50–75 g caster sugar
2 egg yolks, beaten
4 dessertspoons fresh breadcrumbs
¼ pint/150 ml double cream
1 dessertspoon orange juice

❖ Wash the damsons and core and slice the apples. Melt the butter in a saucepan with 2½ fl oz/60 ml water. Add the fruit and boil until soft. Remove from the pan and press through a nylon sieve. Put back in the pan and, still off the heat, stir in the sugar, enough to taste. Blend in the beaten egg yolks and breadcrumbs. Stir over a low heat until quite thick. Leave to cool.
❖ Whisk the cream lightly and fold into the fruit purée. Sharpen to taste with orange juice. Spoon the purée into glasses and chill.

SUFFOLK FOURSES CAKE

A traditional lardy bread, served to Suffolk harvesters in the afternoons with sweetened beer. Rich and full of calories, they were welcome after back-breaking toil.

1½ lb/675 g strong plain flour
½ tablespoon salt
2 teaspoons ground mixed spice
6 oz/175 g lard, softened
½ oz/15 g fresh yeast
2 teaspoons sugar
¾ pint/450 ml warm water
6 oz/175 g currants

OVEN: 200°C/400°F/GAS 6

❖ Cream the yeast with the sugar and a little of the warmed water. Sift the flour, salt and spice into a bowl. Rub in the lard and add the creamed yeast mixture. Stir in the remaining water and mix to a smooth, pliable dough.

❖ Knead the dough thoroughly and leave to rise until it has doubled in size. Knock back and knead in the currants.

❖ Shape the dough into loaves and put into 1 lb/ 450 g loaf tins. Leave to rise again then bake for 45 minutes.

We've ploughed and sowed,
We've reaped and mowed,
And we've gathered in the clover.
And every man will take his can
And neatly toss it over.
Now drink, boys, drink, and if you spill
You shall have two, it is our master's
will.

CAMBRIDGESHIRE HARVEST DRINKING SONG

SEPTEMBER 3

Nutting Day

THIS IS THE DAY on which children would traditionally go out into the local woods to gather hazelnuts. The nuts are supposed to be perfectly ripe at this time – in fact this is often later, but before the calendar change, Nutting Day would have occurred later in the month. However 21st September, St. Matthew's Day, is also known as The Devil's Nutting Day, on which day nuts should not be picked. In some parts of the country it was also thought that you should never gather nuts on a Sunday.

Nutting Day was the day on which lacemakers were allowed to light candles to aid their work. They could use candles during winter from this day until Shrove Tuesday in spring.

Old lacemakers, who spent long hours at their pillows, were advised to refresh their tired eyes by bathing them in gin. This apparently stung a little, but enabled workers to continue for at least two more hours. Eye strain and poor light must have meant blindness for some women, who had to work very long hours even to exist.

NUT LOAF

6 oz/175 g butter
6 oz/175 g caster sugar
3 eggs
8 oz/225 g self-raising flour
1 oz/25 g ground almonds
3 oz/75 g mixed chopped nuts
2 tablespoons milk
TO DECORATE
4 tablespoons apricot jam
3 oz/75 g walnut halves
3 oz/75 g whole brazil nuts

OVEN: 170°C/325°F/GAS 3

❖ Beat the butter and caster sugar together until light and fluffy. Beat in the eggs, one at a time, adding 1 tablespoon of the flour with each egg. Stir in the ground almonds and mixed chopped nuts with the rest of the flour. Add 1–2 tablespoons of milk, if necessary, to make a soft consistency.
❖ Turn into a buttered and lined 2 lb/1 kg loaf tin and bake for 1¼–1½ hours. Turn out on to a wire rack to cool slightly.
❖ When the cake is cold, warm the apricot jam and pass through a sieve. Brush half of it on to the warm cake and fix lines of the walnut halves and brazil nuts over the top. Brush with the remaining apricot jam and leave to cool.

SEPTEMBER 29

Michaelmas

ST. MICHAEL, THE ARCHANGEL, was known in the Old Testament as the protector of the Israelites and in the New Testament as the opponent of the Devil. He is the patron saint of soldiers, horses and also the Mount in Cornwall.

As one of the quarter days, Michaelmas has for many centuries been an important time for payment of rents and generally settling up. It was also a time when people could terminate their service and be hired elsewhere at one of the many Hiring Fairs that took place on this day. These Hiring Fairs were sometimes called Mop Fairs, and workers for hire would carry an emblem of their trade – a mop for a maid, a whip for a carter, a straw for a cowman or a crook for a shepherd. This emblem would be swapped with the new employer for a ribbon and a good-will token of a shilling to be spent at the fair.

And when the tenants come to pay their quarter's rent,
They bring some fowls at Midsummer, a dish of fish at Lent.
At Christmas a capon, at Michaelmas a goose,
And somewhat else at New Year's Tide, for fear their lease fly loose!

SOMERSET MICHAELMAS SONG

A roast 'stubble' goose – rich from its diet of corn and barley gleanings – used to be the customary dish on Michaelmas Day. The tradition probably arose because goose is at its best at this time of year.

Goose fairs used to be held on this day, and still are in many areas although the original reasons for them, selling geese, have long been forgotten. Geese were walked to the famous fairs, often over incredibly long distances. In the 16th century, it is recorded that over twenty thousand geese were taken to the Nottingham Goose Fair and that they were taken on foot from as far as Lincolnshire and Norfolk, their feet having been prepared for the long journey with a mixture of tar and sand.

Whoever eats goose on Michaelmas Day Shall never lack money for his debts to pay.

TRADITIONAL

ROAST GOOSE WITH APPLE AND WALNUT STUFFING

Goose served at this time of year is much less fatty than that available at Christmas, so it can be cooked without the need for basting and boiling water. Allow at least 1 lb/450 g of raw flesh per person.

1 goose
1 lb/450 g cooking apples
1 teaspoon sugar
4 oz/100 g fresh breadcrumbs
1 oz/25 g chopped walnuts
2 teaspoons finely grated onion
Salt and black pepper
1 egg, beaten

OVEN: 180°C/350°F/GAS 4

❖ Wipe over the goose with a damp cloth.
❖ Peel, core and grate the apples. Combine with the sugar, breadcrumbs, walnuts and onion. Season to taste and combine with the beaten egg. Use to stuff the goose.
❖ Place the goose in a roasting tin and prick the skin all over with a skewer. Rub with salt.
❖ Roast the goose for 15 minutes per 1 lb/450 g, plus an additional 15 minutes. Do not baste, but drain off excess fat as necessary. Remove to a warm serving plate and allow to rest until ready to carve.

SORREL SAUCE

❖ Wash 1 lb/450 g sorrel and remove the tough spines. Cook in 1 oz/25 g butter for 5 minutes. Sieve or liquidize, thinned with a little chicken stock if necessary. Reheat and stir in seasoning and a little sugar if desired. Blend in 2 tablespoons double cream and serve hot.

HOT BAKED WARDENS

In Bedfordshire, a two-day fair was held, a feature of which was the sale of baked pears, sold directly from large earthenware dishes. These baked pears were known as wardens.

6 large firm pears
½–¾ pint/300–450 ml red wine
1 oz/25 g brown sugar
Pinch of ground cinnamon, ginger and saffron

OVEN: 180°C/350°F/GAS 4

❖ Peel the pears and place in an ovenproof dish. Mix the red wine with the brown sugar and spices, and pour over the pears. Bake in the oven for 20–30 minutes until tender.

Smoking hot, piping hot
Who knows what I've got
In my pot? Hot baked wardens
All hot! All hot! All hot!

BAKED PEAR VENDOR'S CRY

*I*n the mid-17th century, small cottages in Dorset *would have housed a local industry – that of button-making. These buttons were stitched over felted woollen moulds, using white linen thread. In 1841, the invention of a machine to mechanise this procedure caused the cottage industry to decline and produced a great deal of hardship in rural areas. In Leek, in Staffordshire, buttons were made in coloured silks and this method was also used in parts of Scotland.*

October

St. Faith's Day

St. faith was a 2nd-century christian with two sisters called Hope and Charity. All three sisters, with their mother, were martyred by Emperor Hadrian, for which they were made saints.

In many parts of England, the funeral processions of unmarried girls (or even bachelors) were marked by the carrying of special garlands of white flowers. After the service these garlands would be hung on the beams of the church, often with a pair of white gloves worn by a coffin-bearer to symbolise the purity of the deceased. These garlands used to hang for three Sundays before they were taken down, but in one church, Abbots Ann in Hampshire, these garlands are still hung as a permanent memorial in the church, and new 'maiden garlands' are dedicated annually on St. Faith's Day (6th October).

O good St. Faith, be kind tonight
And bring to me my heart's delight;
Let me my future husband view
And be my vision chaste and true.

ENGLISH FOLK RHYME

ELDERBERRY WINE

This wine can be made with any berries or currants.

6 lb/2.5 kg elderberries
1 gallon/4.5 litres boiling water
3 lb/1.5 kg sugar
2 fl oz/50 ml lemon juice
1 teaspoon fresh yeast

❖ Take the berries off the stalks and check they are insect-free. Put them in a deep bowl and pour on the boiling water. Mash hard with a potato masher, cover and leave for 24 hours. Add the sugar, juice and yeast and leave to ferment (the longer the better). When it has finished fermenting, rack the wine into bottles to leave the sediment behind and store.

Devil's Blackberry Day

OCTOBER 10TH IS THE DAY in folklore on which you are not supposed to pick any more blackberries, as it was once thought that the Devil spits on them today, making them poisonous. The custom arose because 10th October used to be St. Michael's Day before the calendar change in 1752, and there is a legend that when St. Michael threw the Devil out of heaven, the latter landed in a blackberry bush. Perhaps he decided to get his own revenge on blackberry pickers on this day.

In fact blackberries are beginning to be past their best at this time of the year, when the mornings are starting to turn cold and the berries become damp and tempting to insects. In defiance of the Devil, blackberries were cleverly picked the day *before* in some areas, and then made into a special tart or jelly today.

If you do go out to pick blackberries, always try to find those growing away from busy roads. The berries found on the banks of busy highways are contaminated with exhaust fumes and are not as wholesome as one might think.

Season of mists and mellow fruitfulness,
Close bosom-friend of the maturing sun;
Conspiring with him how to load and bless
With fruit the vines that round the thatch eves run.

JOHN KEATS
ODE TO AUTUMN

BRAMBLE JELLY

4 lb/2 kg blackberries
¾ pint/450 ml water
Juice of 2 large lemons
1 lb/450 g sugar to every pint/600 ml of blackberry juice (about 3–4 lb/1.5–2 kg)

❖ Put the blackberries in a pan with the water and lemon juice and simmer until tender. Pour into a muslin jelly bag and leave to drip overnight. (Do not squeeze the bag or the blackberry pulp will escape and cloud the finished jelly.)

❖ Measure the juice, bring to the boil and add 1 lb/450 g warm sugar for every pint/600 ml of juice. Stir until the sugar has dissolved, then boil rapidly until setting point is reached. (This should take about 10 minutes.) Test with a jam thermometer, 105°C/220°F, or for jelling on a saucer.

❖ Pour the jelly into sterilised dry jars and cover.

It is also thought in parts of Cornwall that the weather on October 10th will determine that of the winter to come. If it is warm or windy the winter will be mild, if it is wet, then the winter will be a stormy one.

OCTOBER 17

St. Audrey's Day

A FAIR WAS ONCE HELD at St. Audrey's chapel in Ely to celebrate the Feast of St. Audrey on this day. At the various stalls it was usual for a cheap variety of bobbin lace to be sold. This was of such poor quality that any poor lace was eventually known as St. Audrey's. This in time became shortened to 'tawdry' and this is, apparently, where the term which refers to anything that is cheap and nasty comes from.

One time I gave thee a paper of pins
Another time a tawdry lace
And if thou wilt not grant me love
In truth I'll die before thy face.

ANON

SLOE GIN

IF YOU KNOW WHERE TO FIND WILD SLOES, now is the time to make this warming liqueur for Christmas. It is delicious and perfect to drink by the fire on cold winter evenings.

Sloes can be found in country lanes at this time of year. It is best to wait until the first frosts before gathering sloes, as the frosts will soften their skins and this will result in a better flavoured liqueur. If you cannot find sloes, damsons will make an acceptable substitute.

Gather your sloes, about 2 lb/1 kg. Wash and dry them, and prick each one with a fork or skewer. Put them, with 4–6 oz/100–175 g sugar, into a clean wide-topped jar. The jar should be roughly half full. Top up with a bottle of gin and seal the top down well.

Store the sloe gin for 3 months, giving the jar an occasional shake. When ready strain and bottle. The liqueur makes a delicious drink, and the drained fruit is excellent with ice-cream or custard, and can be frozen until required.

LAST THURSDAY IN OCTOBER

Punkie Night

THIS IS A FESTIVAL particular to the region around Hinton St. George in Somerset. Though its form is similar to some of the goings-on associated with Hallowe'en and Mischief Night in other parts of the country, the origins of Punkie Night are told in a local story. A group of Hinton men apparently once got drunk at a nearby fair on this night, and were unable to find their way home. The women of the parish went out to round up their inebriated husbands, taking punkie lanterns to guide their way.

The punkie is a lantern made from a mangel-wurzel. The lanterns' designs are often extremely elaborate, and not usually so frightening as those created for Hallowe'en. The children of the village spend the days preceding Punkie Night making their lanterns. Unlike pumpkins, they don't scoop out all the flesh but leave a thin layer behind the skin, which they peel off rather than cut through when carving out their designs. As the song here suggests, at one time the children used to go from house to house collecting candles for their lanterns, but now they tend to collect money. On Punkie Night itself, the children parade through the village with their lanterns lit, singing the Punkie Night song.

PUMPKIN SOUP

1½ oz/40 g butter
2 large onions, peeled and sliced
1 lb/450 g potatoes, chopped
2 pints/1.2 litres chicken stock
Salt and black pepper
1 lb/450 g pumpkin flesh, diced
A little cream or butter

❖ Melt the butter in a large saucepan and soften the onions in it. Add the potatoes and sauté for 2–3 minutes. Pour in the stock, season with salt and pepper then add the diced pumpkin. Bring to the boil and simmer until the vegetables are quite tender.

❖ Remove the pan from the heat, cool slightly and rub through a fine sieve or liquidise. Reheat if necessary, season to taste and stir in a little cream or butter.

It's Punkie Night tonight,
It's Punkie Night tonight
Give us a candle, give us a light,
If you don't you'll get a fright.

CHILDREN'S CHANT

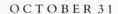

OCTOBER 31

Hallowe'en

THIS IS THE NIGHT when the dead are said to rise from their graves, and witches, goblins and other dreaded beings are thought to be at their most active. It is a time for mischief and magic, shrouded in mysteries and superstition from the depths of time.

Traditionally, Hallowe'en is a night for staying by the fire, out of harm's way, and telling fortunes. In some areas, fires were lit on hillsides to ward off evil spirits and stones were thrown into the flames. The next day, people searched amongst the ashes to find their stones and be assured of good fortune. If stones were not recovered, it meant misfortune or even death. In other areas, nuts were thrown on the fire and meanings were given to the different ways they burned. If a nut burned brightly, it meant that the thrower would still be alive in twelve months time. If it flared up suddenly with a bright light, it meant marriage within twelve months.

There is an old belief that you can ascertain the initials of a future lover by peeling an apple on Hallowe'en, keeping the peel intact and throwing it over your shoulder. The form it takes is said to be that of the loved one's initials.

In Scotland, it was common practice to make Fortune-Telling Pudding, into which small silver charms would be stirred. In some areas this took the form of a steamed fruit pudding, in other areas it was more like a porridge known as Crowdie. Each guest would take a spoonful of Crowdie in turn until they recovered a charm. Each charm was assigned a meaning, and a member of the house with second sight would offer an interpretation.

On Hallowe'en the old ghosts come
About us – and they speak to some.

ANON

FORTUNE-TELLING CROWDIE

2 heaped tablespoons oatmeal, lightly toasted
½ pint/300 ml double cream, lightly whipped
1 oz/25 g caster sugar, to taste
1 tablespoon rum

❖ Combine the oatmeal with the whipped cream and stir in the sugar to taste.
❖ Add the rum then chill slightly.
❖ Just before serving, stir in some charms and pour into a bowl. Each guest is then asked to take a spoonful in turn until they bring out a charm.

A coin for wealth
A ring for marriage
A button for a bachelor
A thimble for a spinster
A wishbone for your heart's desire

HALLOWE'EN CHARMS

CRUMPETS (PIKELETS)

This recipe will make 12 crumpets.

2 tablespoons oil
½ pint/300 ml lukewarm milk
½ pint/300 ml lukewarm water
½ oz/15 g fresh or ½ tablespoon dried yeast
1 teaspoon soft brown sugar
8 oz/225 g strong white flour
8 oz/225 g white plain flour
1 tablespoon salt
½ teaspoon bicarbonate of soda
¼ pint/150 ml warm water

❖ Warm the oil in a bowl in a low oven and then add the milk and water.
❖ Cream the yeast with the sugar then gradually blend in the mixed liquids. Stand until frothy.
❖ Combine the flours in a bowl and warm slightly in a low oven. Mix in the salt then stir in the yeast liquid. Beat well. Cover with a damp cloth and leave to rise for about 2 hours. Beat down vigorously with a wooden spoon.
❖ Mix the bicarbonate of soda with the warm water and stir into the batter mixture. Cover and leave to rise again in a warm place for about 30 minutes.
❖ Lightly grease crumpet rings and griddle (or a heavy-based frying pan), and heat the griddle slowly. Place the rings on the griddle and pour enough batter into each to half fill them.
❖ Cook gently over a low heat for 10 minutes until a skin has formed on the top. Remove the rings and turn the crumpets over to brown the top surface. Cook for a further 3–4 minutes, then put on to a warm plate and cover with a napkin. Serve with plenty of butter.

MASH OF NINE SORTS

In some rural areas, it was usual at Hallowe'en supper to serve a 'Mash of Nine Sorts' to unmarried guests, in which the lady of the house would have hidden her wedding ring. The lucky finder would be the first of the guests to find a partner. Originally there were just the 'nine' ingredients – but I have added cheese and butter to make it tastier.

1 lb/450 g potatoes
2 carrots
1 turnip
1 parsnip
Salt and pepper
A little single cream
3–4 oz/75–100 g cheese, grated
2 oz/50 g butter
2 leeks
4 oz/100 g cooked peas

OVEN: 180°C/350°F/GAS 4

❖ Peel all the vegetables (except the peas) and either halve (in the case of the potatoes) or slice. Boil the potatoes in one pan of salted water until tender, and the carrots, turnip and parsnip in another. Drain the potatoes and the other vegetables and put them both into a large bowl.

❖ Mash the vegetables together and then press through a sieve. Season to taste. Beat in the single cream and half of the grated cheese.

❖ Melt the butter in a frying pan and gently fry the finely sliced leeks until golden brown. Tip the leeks and butter into the mashed vegetable, and season with lots of black pepper and a little salt. Stir in the cooked peas and transfer to an earthenware dish.

❖ Sprinkle with the remaining cheese and cook for 40 minutes until golden brown and bubbling.

*I*n Scotland, 'guising' is traditional on Hallowe'en, which is often referred to there as Mischief Night. Children dress up and disguise themselves, and go from house to house collecting apples, nuts and sweets. Sometimes the children have to earn the goodies by performing a party piece, and the households they visit have to guess who they are disguised as. Similar customs have been introduced to the rest of the country via America, where it is known as 'trick or treat'.

Heigh ho for hallowe'en
When the fairies a' are seen,
Some black and some green
Heigh ho for hallowe'en.

TRADITIONAL

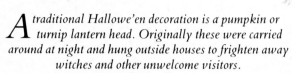

A traditional Hallowe'en decoration is a pumpkin or turnip lantern head. Originally these were carried around at night and hung outside houses to frighten away witches and other unwelcome visitors.

To make a pumpkin or turnip lantern, cut a slice from the top of the vegetable and scoop out the flesh. (If using a pumpkin, reserve for the soup recipe on page 109.) After removing the flesh, cut out the eyes, nose and mouth and shape triangular ears at either side. Hollow out the lid, place a night-light candle inside the head and cover with the lid. The candle should burn all evening.

From ghoulies and ghosties and long-legged beasties
And things that go bump in the night,
Good Lord, deliver us!

CORNISH PRAYER

November

All Saints' Day

ALL SAINTS' DAY on 1st November commemorates the saints and martyrs of the Christian faith, and used to be an important date in the Christian calendar. It is also known as All Hallows' Day, as 'hallow' means 'saint' in Old English.

November 1st is also All Souls' Eve, the time when families remember the souls of departed relatives, thought to return to their old homes on this night. Prayers were said for the dead, and food left on kitchen tables in the night. 'Souling' would also take place, where soulers would travel from door to door begging for soul-cakes in return for songs and prayers. This custom was spread in various parts of the country over the three days of Hallowe'en, All Saints' Day and All Souls' Day.

No shade, no shine, no butterflies, no bees,
No fruits, no flowers, no leaves, no birds
– November!

THOMAS HOOD
NO!

HARCAKE

In Lancashire, this was offered to visitors on All Saints' Day.

1 lb/450 g fine oatmeal
2 oz/50 g butter, softened
½ oz/15 g ground ginger
12 oz/350 g golden syrup
1 egg, beaten
A little brown ale

OVEN: 180°C/350°F/GAS 4

❖ Rub the butter into the oatmeal. Add the ginger and stir in the syrup. Beat in the egg and add a little ale. Grease a tin and pour in the mixture.

❖ Bake for about 1–1½ hours until firm. Cool and then cut into squares. When cold, wrap in greaseproof paper and store in an airtight container. Keep for a week before eating.

All Souls' Day

ALL SOULS' DAY (like All Saints' Day and Hallowe'en) has its origins in the ancient Celtic Feast of the Dead, called Samhain. On this day, prayers were once said for souls in purgatory. It was kept as a solemn fast day and often bonfires were lit on the hills at night to light the souls' way – in many Latin countries, people also used to put candles in churchyards and cemeteries.

The poor of the village used to offer their richer neighbours their prayers for departed relatives in return for alms or soul-cakes. This custom became ritualised, and practised by many members of the village. Special souling songs were sung, and sometimes a souling play performed. The traditional drink served to soulers (or 'cakers' as they were sometimes known) was spiced ale, which must have been very welcome during a cold November walk around the village. Apples, sweets and even money as well as soul-cakes used to be collected by soulers.

Traditionally, the following lines were spoken just before a soul-cake was eaten:

A soul-cake, a soul-cake
Have mercy, lord, on all Christian souls.

TRADITIONAL

SOUL-CAKES

6 oz/175 g butter
6 oz/175 g caster sugar
3 egg yolks
1 lb/450 g plain flour
1 teaspoon ground mixed spice
3 oz/75 g currants
A little milk, to mix

OVEN: 180°C/350°F/GAS 4

❖ Cream the butter and sugar together in a bowl then beat in the egg yolks, one at a time. Sift the flour and spice into another bowl then add to the butter mixture. Stir in the currants, and add milk if necessary to form a soft dough.

❖ Form the dough into flat cakes and mark each with a cross. Put on to a greased baking sheet and bake for 10–15 minutes until golden brown.

A soul, a soul, a soul cake,
Please good missus a soul cake,
An apple, a pear, a plum or a cherry,
Or any good thing to make us merry.

OLD SOULERS' RHYME

SPICED ALE

2 pints/1.2 litres real ale
Pinch of ground cloves
Pinch of ground ginger
Pinch of ground allspice
Cinnamon stick
4 fl oz/125 ml brandy
1 tablespoon soft, brown sugar

❖ Put the ale and spices into a large saucepan and bring almost to boiling point. Take from the heat and stir in the brandy and sugar. Serve at once.

NOVEMBER 5

Guy Fawkes' Day

THIS DAY COMMEMORATES the failure of the plot in 1605 by Guido (Guy) Fawkes, Robert Catesby, Thomas Winter and others to blow up King James I and his parliament.

The capturing of the plotters has been celebrated ever since on this day with large bonfires and firework displays, which over the years have generally become municipal rather than household events.

Guy Fawkes' Day is marked by many fire-related customs, some particularly boisterous and even dangerous. In Ottery St. Mary, in Devon, huge ignited barrels of tar are borne blazing through the town at breakneck speed, and home-made 'cannons' are set off at dawn to wake up the whole town. In some parts of the country, especially in the North, Guy Fawkes' Eve is also known as Mischief Night, an excuse for many pranks and minor lawlessness.

TOM TROT TOFFEE

In Yorkshire a treacle toffee is made on Guy Fawkes' Night with the curious name of Tom Trot.

1 lb/450 g soft brown sugar
5 tablespoons water
2 teaspoons vinegar
1 oz/25 g butter
¼ pint/150 ml black treacle

❖ Put the sugar into a saucepan with the water and vinegar and when dissolved add the butter and the treacle. Heat gently until the butter and treacle melt. Raise the heat and boil for 12–15 minutes. The temperature on a sugar thermometer should read 138°C–142°C/280°F–290°F.

❖ Pour the treacle into an oiled tin and leave until partially set. Mark into bars or squares and, when cold, break up and store in an airtight tin.

Please to remember
The fifth of November
Gunpowder, treason and plot.
I see no reason
Why gunpowder treason
Should ever be forgot.

ANON

NOVEMBER 11

Martinmas

St. martin of tours was a cavalry soldier before he became a monk. He was renowned for his charity and humility, and his ability to bring light to those who lived in the shadow of despair. He is now known as the patron saint of beggars, drunkards and outcasts.

St. Martin's feast day is now celebrated much more in France than in this country, but before industrialisation, it was one of the high spots on the farm worker's calendar and remained so until the 1920s in parts of northern England. As a quarter day, it was a time for collecting rents and paying debts as well as being one of the main times for hiring and finding better employment at the hiring fairs held around the country.

Martinmas used to be one of the major feast days, particularly as people were often receiving payments and could afford to celebrate and share with family and friends. It was also the time when many animals were slaughtered and salted down for the winter.

Today, Martinmas marks a more sombre occasion – Remembrance Day. Now, on the Sunday nearest to the 11th November, church services are held in memory of those who died in World Wars I and II, and red poppies are worn in commemoration.

MARTINMAS BEEF

3 lb/1.5 g brisket of beef
1 inch/2.5 cm piece of root ginger
2–3 blades of mace
¼ nutmeg, grated
¼ teaspoon ground cloves
1 teaspoon salt
½ pint/300 ml dry white wine
2 tablespoons white wine vinegar
1 oz/25 g cornflour

OVEN: 140°C/275°F/GAS 1

❖ Put the beef into an earthenware casserole dish. Finely chop the ginger root and mix with mace, grated nutmeg, cloves and salt. Stir the spices into the wine with the vinegar. Pour over the beef.

❖ Cover with a tight-fitting lid and cook in the oven for 3–4 hours. Remove the meat to a warm plate. Thicken the sauce in a pan with the cornflour, first mixed with a little cold water to make a smooth paste. Heat the sauce until it thickens and serve with the beef.

NOVEMBER 23

St. Clement's Day

ST. CLEMENT WAS A CHRISTIAN MARTYR who died in the 4th century by being thrown out to sea weighed to an anchor. He is the patron saint of blacksmiths, and his feast day was a popular event in the calendar until quite recently. On his day blacksmiths used to parade around the countryside carrying an effigy of St. Clement, which they called 'Old Clem'. The image was used to beg alms (called 'clementing'), and the money collected was used for a local feast. Clem Suppers were common in many parts of Sussex, Kent and Hampshire, and a toast was always made to the blacksmiths.

Clementing was also popular among children in the Midlands, who would carry an 'Old Clem' around and sing clementing songs in return for apples or special spiced cakes.

The apple-paring game associated with Hallowe'en was also once practised by children on 23rd November, as was the game of apple-bobbing, from which St. Clement's Day received its other name of Bite Apple Day.

Clementing cakes were traditionally sold at the Clementide Sheep Fair once held at this time in Berkshire.

ST. CLEMENT'S TARTLETS

8 oz/225 g shortcrust pastry (see page 22)
1 orange
1 lemon
3 oz/75 g butter, softened
3 oz/75 g sugar
2 eggs, separated
¼ teaspoon vanilla essence

OVEN: 200°C/400°F/GAS 6

❖ Roll out the pastry and use to line individual tartlet tins. Carefully remove the rinds from the orange and the lemon and chop very finely.

❖ Cream the butter and the sugar together in a bowl. Beat the egg yolks and gradually stir into the creamed butter and sugar mixture.

❖ Squeeze the orange and add 2 tablespoons of its juice to the mixture. Stir in the citrus rinds and the vanilla essence.

❖ Whisk the egg whites until stiff and fold into the rest of the ingredients.

❖ Pour into pastry cases and bake in the oven for 25 minutes. Cool on a wire rack.

SUNDAY BEFORE ADVENT

Stir-up Sunday

Stir up, we beseech thee, O Lord, the wills of thy faithful people; that they, plenteously bringing forth the fruit of good works, may be of thee plenteously rewarded.

THE COLLECT FOR THE 25TH SUNDAY AFTER TRINITY, BOOK OF COMMON PRAYER

CONGREGATIONS TOOK THE EXHORTATION to 'Stir up' to be a reminder that the time had arrived to make their Christmas puddings so that they would have time to mature well for Christmas. It was also believed that puddings made on this day would carry God's blessings to all who partook of it.

Christmas pudding originated in the 16th century as a plum porridge made of meat broth, fruit juice, wine, prunes, mace and breadcrumbs, which was served in a semi-liquid state. In the late 17th century it began to solidify and by the 18th century it was simply rolled into a ball, wrapped in a cloth and boiled. The Victorians introduced the idea of boiling it in a basin.

Stir up, we beseech thee
The pudding in the pot
And when we get home
We'll eat it all hot!

CHOIRBOYS' RHYME

CHRISTMAS PUDDING

Lucky charms and rings used to be put into the pudding, or you could add a lucky sixpenny piece if you have one. When making a pudding, each member of the family should take a turn in the stirring and make a wish. You must stir clockwise, the direction in which the sun was assumed to proceed around the earth. To stir anti-clockwise has always been considered unlucky.

TO MAKE 2 LARGE PUDDINGS

1 lb/450 g raisins
8 oz/225 g currants
8 oz/225 g sultanas
2 oz/50 g fresh dates
2 oz/50 g crystallised fruit (see page 13)
2 oz/50 g flaked almonds
½ teaspoon freshly grated nutmeg
½ teaspoon ground mixed spice
½ teaspoon ground cinnamon
2 oz/50 g ground almonds
1 teaspoon salt
12 oz/350 g fresh brown breadcrumbs
4 oz/100 g soft brown sugar
1 lb/450 g butter, softened
6 large eggs, beaten
4 tablespoons brandy or rum
8 fl oz/225 ml stout

❖ Mince the dried fruit, crystallized fruit and the flaked almonds. Mix together with all the dried fruit, spices, ground almonds and salt. Blend thoroughly.

❖ Work in the breadcrumbs, sugar and softened butter. Stir the beaten eggs into the mixture together with the brandy and stout, to make a soft dropping consistency.

❖ Butter two large pudding bowls and spoon half the mixture into both. Cover with greaseproof paper and pudding cloths and tie down.

❖ Boil steadily in open pans for 6 hours, topping up the water level when necessary with hot water, or steam in a pressure-cooker according to the manufacturer's instructions.

❖ Remove the cloths and cover the puddings with fresh greaseproof paper. Store in a cool place. On Christmas Day, boil for a further 4 hours.

Stem the currants
Stone the raisins
Chop the peel as fine as fine
Beat the eggs and shred the suet
Grate the crumbs (no flour in mine)
Freely shake, to make it nice,
All the virtue of the spice.
Pour the brandy liberally.
Stir and wish, then, three times three.

ELEANOR FARJEON
STIRRING THE PUDDING

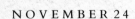

NOVEMBER 24

St. Catherine's Eve

DURING THE EVENING on St. Catherine's Eve, lacemakers often used to prepare a 'Cathern Bowl'. Apples would be roasted before an open fire, suspended by strings from the beams, until the apple pulp fell into a bowl of cider spiced with sugar and cinnamon set beneath it. When all the apple pulp was successfully caught and mixed, it would be strained and offered to guests. Fortified with this brew, young lacemakers would then jump the candlesticks for luck. A lighted candle was placed on the floor and each girl would jump over it – if she extinguished the flame, then ill-luck would follow her for the rest of the year. The belief that flame could purify one's life and that by passing through fire luck could be changed is an ancient one.

Kit be nimble, Kit be quick
Kit jump over the candlestick.

LACEMAKER'S RHYME

As we approach the end of the book, the Eve of St. Catherine's seems an appropriate 'Cutting Off Day'. For lacemakers, Cutting Off Day was when they cut off and sold the lace they had made. Originally, lacemakers would produce only one pattern, with which they had become conversant. This would have been worked in one continuous piece – corners being a relatively modern innovation (corners were formed by easing and gathering the lace to fit the garment) and, on Cutting Off Day the lace dealer would take the lace from each pillow and pay according to the length produced. In many areas fine lace would be paid for by the shilling – the lace would be covered with one shilling pieces and the lacemaker was paid the amount thus arrived at.

Here the needle plies its busy task,
The pattern grows, the well-depicted
flower,
Wrought patiently into the snowy lawn,
Unfolds its bosom, buds and leaves and
sprigs;
And curling tendrils, gracefully disposed,
Follow the nimble fingers of the fair.
A wreath that cannot fade of flowers that
blow,
With most success when all besides decay.

COWPER
A WINTER'S EVENING

There I will make thee beds of roses
And a thousand fragrant posies,
A cap of flowers, and a kirtle
Embroider'd all with leaves of myrtle.

A gown made of the finest wool,
Which from our pretty lambs we pull,
Fair lin'd slippers for the cold,
With buckles of the purest gold.

Thy silver dishes for thy meat,
As precious as the gods do eat,
Shall on an ivory table be
Prepared each day for thee and me.

CHRISTOPHER MARLOWE
THE PASSIONATE SHEPHERD TO HIS LOVE

Never mind about the piece
of needlework, the tambouring,
the maps of the world made
by her needle – get to see her
at work upon a mutton chop.

WILLIAM COBBETT
ADVICE TO YOUNG MEN

Epilogue

The year has turned full circle and we find ourselves once more looking towards the celebration of Christmas and the beginning of a new year. Life for us today is no more certain than it was for our predecessors and yet we, like them, can take comfort in the promise that each season brings. Let us continue to serve shortbread and whisky for the New Year, pancakes on Shrove Tuesday and eggs for Easter. Each one of us can expand and enjoy the simple pleasures that these rituals bring and the warmth and security that goes with the keeping of these age-old customs.

Index

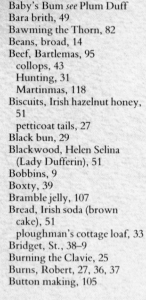

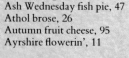

Bibliography and Acknowledgements

British Calendar Customs, Wright & Lones (The Folklore Society, 1936)

Food in England, Dorothy Hartley (Macdonald, 1954)

English Bread and Yeast Cookery, Elizabeth David (Penguin, 1977)

Traditional English Foods, Cathie Webber (Batsford, 1981)

A Calendar of Country Customs, Ralph Whitlock (Batsford, 1978)

The Winter Solstice, Shirley Toulson (Jill Norman & Hobhouse, 1981)

The Lore and Language of Schoolchildren, Iona and Peter Opie (Paladin, 1982)

Dictionary of Christian Lore and Legend, J. C. J. Metford (Thames & Hudson, 1983)

History of Lace, Mrs Bury Paliffer (Dover Publications, 1984)

The National Trust Guide to Traditional Customs of Britain, Brian Shuel (Webb & Bower, 1985)

The Customs and Ceremonies of Britain, Charles Kightly (Thames & Hudson, 1986)

THE AUTHORS WOULD LIKE TO THANK
The curator and staff of The County Museum at Shugborough Hall for their help, and Keith Brandrick for his help and patience in obtaining obscure cuts of meat and goose feathers! Also, Anita Toothill for the loan of her Honiton lace butterfly, Mr and Mrs Norman Burton for the loan of postcards, Mrs B Smith for her sample of smocking, Birmingham Reference Library for permission to reproduce pictures from the Benjamin Stone Collection, and all our friends who have contributed advice, recipes and information.

We would also like to thank Jean Withers and Joyce Jones, Batsford Ltd, for permission to reproduce their lace designs, and Faber & Faber for permission to reproduce part of the Ballad of the Mari Lwyd by Vernon Watkins.

THE PUBLISHERS WOULD LIKE TO THANK
Katy Sleight for the illustrated backgrounds of this book, Catherine Treasure and Carolyn Ryden for additional research, and Jill Foster for testing recipes.